FRANK SELVY

Coal Miner's Son

Book design by Caryn Scheving
Printed in Anderson, SC by PIP Marketing Signs Print

For more information about this book, please write the author at
2802 High Shoals Road
Anderson, SC 29621
or email jackmackt@aol.com

Frank Selvy: Coal Miner's Son can be ordered from amazon.com

FRANK SELVY

Coal Miner's Son

By Jack McIntosh

Table of Contents

Foreword

This book is about basketball…and a lot more. It's about a 12-year-old boy who forfeited his childhood and went into a coal mine to support his family. This is poverty and hardship of the first dimension. A 12-year-old boy doesn't earn a merit badge in the coal mine, and he never experiences the joyful sounds of the playground, and he never learns games. This is what happened to Frank Selvy's father, and it shaped Frank's life. Despite great fame, he remains to this day a coal miner's son.

Who is Frank Selvy?

Teammates and classmates know a person well from close association and experiences.

Jerry West, who was a teammate with the Los Angeles Lakers, has this to say:

When I first joined the Los Angeles Lakers in the 1960s, little did I know that I would meet someone that shared a childhood and upbringing that was so similar to mine; I felt that Frank was more of a brother than a teammate. We shared a great love of the game of basketball. Our fathers were both coal miners and I'm certain that it's been well documented how harsh and difficult their occupations were. We were taught respect and the value of being good and productive citizens.

Frank and I were quiet until engaged. We both loved to

compete and we valued our teammates with whom we shared many stories of our growing up and of our families. Frank loved golf, a game he introduced me to, and he shared with me his knowledge of this great game that I still enjoy today. He also introduced me and our teammates to card games while on road trips. I will always cherish those enjoyable moments that we all shared.

Frank and his wife Barbara have always been a great couple and they were so good to my family; words cannot express how much they have meant to me over the years since we met.

Frank elevated the game and was always a fan favorite. Everyone knew of his offense and his 100-point game in college but it didn't take long to realize what a strong defender he was; his all-around play was a great value to our Lakers team.

I was blessed to have Frank as a teammate and so enjoyed our days together; he was a great credit to the game. He was a terrific player and even a better man and a loyal, lifelong friend.

Richard W. "Dick" Riley, former South Carolina governor and former U.S. Secretary of Education, added this from his perspective as a classmate at Furman University:

For us at Furman, Frank Selvy will always be our All-American graduate. He made his mark on Furman and still makes us proud of our friend and classmate. This is a real story about our country and the opportunities it gives us if one works hard and overcomes barriers to use his talents for good purposes.

A youngster with talent needs both character and determination if he wants to go to the top. Talent and determination will produce the skills and success, but character will determine how to react to the honors and rewards that success provides. There are two sides to the hill and little room at the top. A player hears a lot of cheers from the crowd as he ascends and even more when he arrives at the peak and is challenged to find room on his mantel for all the trophies. It's when he begins to see the downside of the hill that his character is called upon. It becomes lonely in the quiet room that follows success. Time to quit? A man who gained his strength from a Bible-reading mother and the dedicated work ethic learned from a coal miner father doesn't quit—or cheat or complain. All of these things the reader should take away from this book.

Frank Selvy and his wife Barbara were rewarded in many ways but they were not spared the pain and disappointments others endure. Of all the rewards they received, none have they appreciated more than the lasting friendships established while Frank was a student athlete at Furman University, the member of a basketball team that electrified the sports world. These are friends who have remained constant for more than sixty years and still are happy to relate stories about the time when Frank Selvy was the best in the basketball world and they were the supporting cast. Teammate Bobby Chambers said it well: "Frank would be my friend even if he never saw a basketball."

These friends continued to have an impact on basketball for many years. Frank Selvy's jersey and number 28 are displayed at the Timmons Arena on the Furman University campus, where it hangs from the ceiling as a reminder of a great decade for Furman's

Paladins. After his professional career, Frank served as the Paladins' assistant coach for two years and head coach for four years. His teammate Nield Gordon, who also played as a professional, later coached as an assistant at Furman and head coach at Winthrop University and Newberry College. Nield was the Winthrop coach when the female college began admitting men, and took the Winthrop team to the playoffs.) Bobby Roberts, another teammate, became head basketball coach at Clemson University.

The history of basketball is made up of many such stories as this, telling how each generation produces players who honor the game and improve it with some unique contribution. Frank Selvy introduced the jump shot to basketball and established scoring records that were unbelievable at the time. Those of us who love sports all have our sports heroes--but not all great athletes are great role models. For this reason alone, Frank should be remembered. I hope this book will help establish his name as one of the truly great players of the game.

The great English poet A.E. Housman wrote:

And now you will not swell the route of lads who wore their
honors out;
Runners who renown outran, and the name died before the man.

These lines could have been written about Frank Selvy, the coal miner's son.

Jack McIntosh
Anderson, SC
January 2016

1

The Boy from Kentucky

Basketball was a secondary sport on college campuses in the late 1940s and the one at Furman University, a private liberal arts school in Greenville, South Carolina, a textile town, was in a slump. Furman's program was suffering the effects of a low budget fueled largely with ticket sales and the challenge of recovering from years when the eligible young players had traded shooting hoops for shooting guns in the battlefields of World War II. Coach Lyles Alley, himself a veteran, had taken a leave of absence to pursue a master's degree at Columbia University, perhaps with an eye toward a career change.

That all began to change one day in 1949 when a carload of young men from Kentucky drove onto campus to meet with Furman Athletic Director Jim Meade and Interim Basketball Coach Melvin Bell. One of the recruits was Frank Selvy.

Bell recalled that Meade told him to take the young men into the gym "to see what they had." Frank was six feet tall and weighed, at most, 150 pounds. He told Bell that he played center, which raised questions in the coach's mind because of his lack of size. "I told him to show me a left-handed hook shot, which he did by arching the ball so that it dropped directly down into the net without touching the backboard." He repeated the left-handed shot on command, and then shot with his dominant right hand. The same result.

"I was impressed," Bell said.

Next he directed one of the other boys to guard Frank, who he asked to use his jump shot. He easily shot over the hands of the guard, dropping a swish shot into the net. Equally impressive. "I directed him to take the ball and score any way he wanted to and that's exactly what he did," Bell remembered. "He could score at will. Driving the basket from either side using his left or right hand to dribble or shoot, he turned the defender into a spectator standing still as he went for his layup."

It was an amazing performance. Bell later said Selvy was, without exception, the best high school player he had ever seen, an opinion that he relayed to Jim Meade. "I also said that he could be All-Southern and quite likely All-American." Unfortunately, Bell as an interim coach was unable to translate his enthusiasm into an offer, and in those days before cell phones, Meade was unable to reach Coach Alley. Selvy and the other Kentucky boys went back home. But when Alley finally reached Selvy, he returned to Furman for good and all of Bell's predictions came true—and then some.

From 1950 to 1954, Frank Selvy would lead the Furman University basketball players to recognition on the national stage. His record-smashing scoring packed fans into arenas at home and on the road, not the least of which was a night in 1954 when he racked up 100 points in one game. Upon graduating in 1954, he was the No. 1 draft pick in the nation, and began a professional career with a then unheard-of contract of $10,000. In current dollars, that's almost $89,000. In comparison, the No. 1 rookie for the 2014-15 class earned a first-year salary of almost $4.6 million.

These figures demonstrate how basketball has risen from "the other sport," greatly lagging football, to a national passion that more than holds its own. Frank Selvy had a role in that transformation.

Yet he remains to this day a quiet, modest, unassuming man who doesn't rehash his victories. He remains to this day what he was from his earliest days in the gritty railroad town of Corbin, Kentucky: a coal miner's son.

2

A Brief History of Appalachia

There is no place in America quite like the Appalachian Plateau. Its people have a long history of living harsh and painful lives in isolated hills and hollows where they struggle to survive. There has been no shortage of studies made on the people of Appalachia and experiments conducted to understand them and improve their living conditions. These good intentions have met with little success, a testament to how futile it is for social and political activists to apply their formulas for change to people who don't want to change and really don't trust outsiders.

Any attempt to understand the Kentucky mountaineers and their code requires going back to the earliest days of the settling of the United States. The need for laborers took agents to the teeming and disease-ridden streets of European cities. There, poverty-stricken men and women contracted for passage to the New World colonies where they willingly submitted to a form of bondage. As indentured servants, they worked without wage to pay back the cost of passage. Not all of them came under contract, because unscrupulous agents would often kidnap laborers and bring them shanghai-fashion into the same situations as their more willing brethren.

Poverty brings out the toughness in people and they learn survival skills if nothing else. When their contract was fulfilled, those who survived often went west into the frontier and many of them ended up in the Appalachian Mountains. Led by frontiersmen like Daniel Boone, they moved into territory dominated by the Choctaw and Cherokee tribes and copied their methods of home building and agriculture, becoming greatly influenced by their customs and ways. They became expert hunter-gatherers and primitive in their life-styles, much like the Indians around them. Initially, the children had no schooling and there were no churches. While there was some intermarriage and other constructive relationships established between the Indians and white settlers, there was also conflict that resulted in the settlers using their long rifles in defense of their cabins and families.

What they had in spades were abundant natural resources. The clear-moving streams and rivers ran through amazing forests of giant oaks, poplars and pines. The tall and straight poplars rose to heights of well over a hundred feet and were of great value to ship builders, among others. Early on, the Kentucky mountaineers found a market for the tall timbers and generated minimal income by cutting and trimming the trees. They stacked them alongside streams until spring when the swollen waters would float the logs down to Frankfurt where they were sold. Timber, along with "shine" whiskey, was the major money crop, but this home-grown industry barely touched the vast virgin forests.

Conflicts with the Indians were not the only ones in these mountains. When the Civil War began in 1861, mountain families were divided. Some wore the blue and some the gray and, in some instances, family members wore both from one time to another. This didn't generate hostility until the word began to come home of deaths of sons, and tolerance for the other side faded fast. Violent feuds began—that of the Hatfields and McCoys being the best known--and continued even after the war ended and other parts of the country had begun to heal. This was due to the fact that families were isolated by the topography of the hills and hollows and they had few distractions from their quest for revenge. One vengeful act led to another, creating a code of mutual destruction.

Deep beneath the ground in these mountains were rich veins of coal and other minerals which, along with the timber, attracted investors from the Northeast. They sent their clever agents into the mountains with "short form" deeds to buy land for as little as 26 cents an acre. When they couldn't buy the land outright, the agents bought timber and mineral rights, leaving the uneducated mountaineer with the right to live on his land and pay taxes until a railroad line was constructed and exfoliation began in earnest. These wholesale logging and mining operations, which began in 1875 and continued for decades, led to slag and waste deposits along with erosion that rendered the land useless and the mountaineers dependent on coal companies.

Initially there was a strong element of good will between the owner/operators and the mountaineer workers, and this continued as long as there was a strong demand for coal and profits and pay were high. But when the economy turned, so did the relationships. The coal miner was a tough individual and the product of a harsh environment. Working for hours with pick and shovel in a dark and dangerous place would have been difficult enough, but the additional hardship of fighting for a reasonable wage and working conditions made him even tougher.

The companies built homes for the families to live in and

commissaries for the purchase of necessities. As the profits dropped, the demands on the workers increased and the cost of goods at the company stores went up. Those who had automobiles were required to purchase gas at the company service station at company prices, and it could cost a miner his job if he shopped elsewhere for gas or other necessities. The situation inspired Merle Travis to write his song "Sixteen Tons":

> *You load sixteen tons and what do you get*
> *Another day older and deeper in debt.*
> *Saint Peter, don't you call me 'cause I can't go,*
> *I owe my soul to the company store.*

In the 1890s, a union called the United Mine Workers was formed to give the miners a common voice in dealing with management. When organizers came to a mining town, the companies hired thugs and goons to drive them out and anyone who talked to an organizer could lose his job. Nevertheless, the union grew under the leadership of John L. Lewis. You can only push people so far and they push back, especially in a part of the country where the code of behavior always favored revenge. That's what happened in Harlan County, Kentucky in the early 1930s when worker's wages were cut 10 percent and the efforts of the UMW resulted in bloody labor unrest that lasted almost a decade.

It was in this dark and violent time that Frank Selvy was born to a miner named James Selvy and his wife, Iva.

3

Daddy Was a Miner

James Selvy was twelve years old when he went into the mines. He had little choice, as his father had been sent to prison for killing a man. The story was that the elder Selvy was wrongfully convicted because he had a hole in his coat said to have been caused by gunshot. It was also said that the victim would have killed him first had he gotten the chance.

It was another example of the harsh code observed by men and women from the hollows and hills. James Selvy's father had two options, neither of them good. If you don't kill him, he will kill you. Either way your son ends up in the mine where he struggles in the dark and dangerous world which kills people. Those it doesn't kill it maims and leaves with soot-filled lungs insufficient to sustain a man. Miners go underground before the sun rises and come up after it sets…bent and stiff from crawling around on their hands and knees as their chests slowly fill with coal dust.

It's the kind of struggle that leads even a good man to a bottle. Such poverty and hardship will often lead gentle women to the Bible and tough men to drink, but gentle women raise strong sons. Such were James and Iva Selvy.

They married when James was thirty and Iva was a very young girl. Frank, the fourth of their ten children, was born on November 9, 1932, the day after Franklin Delano Roosevelt was swept into office by one of the largest margins of victory in American politics. The Selvys named their baby boy Franklin after the new president, and for years he thought his middle name was Delano. He eventually learned it was just "D."

Roosevelt's election and the New Deal brought some easing of hardship in Kentucky in the form of public works projects and food aid. The United Mine Workers had greater success due to labor reforms protecting union activity. But it was the talent and success of Franklin D. Selvy that really lifted his family from poverty.

He shared a birth year with another Kentucky coal miner's child named Loretta Webb. Like Frank, she was raised in a small home with many siblings by a hard-working miner and his Bible-loving wife. After marrying at age fifteen and birthing four babies by the time she was twenty, she became famous as the queen of country music, Loretta Lynn. In her signature song "Coal Miner's Daughter," Lynn pays tribute to parents who made sure their children had love when they didn't have much else.

James Selvy worked in a mine away from the family home in Corbin, best known as the birthplace of the Kentucky Fried Chicken fast food chain. He hopped a train to work during the week, leaving the child-rearing to Iva, and then returned on the weekends, a distant, stern-faced figure who would have a bottle or two to relax. The children kept a low profile when he was home, generally staying outdoors. There wasn't much indoors anyway, for the house was crowded with all the children and just two bedrooms. It was a religious house, where Iva, who was of the Pentecostal Holiness faith, read the Bible to her brood.

What can you say of the father, who was never really allowed to be a boy and who spent most of his life underground hacking and shoveling coal for a living? He was a product of his time and place and should be much respected for providing for his large family during very hard times. He continued to do so until he was injured in a mining accident at age 54 and was forced to retire. After 42 years of digging, he received a pension of $90 a month. James had little time for recreation, and never saw his talented son play basketball until well into his college career.

Like many families who were struggling to put food on the table, the Selvys had a pig. The pig had to be fed and a family with ten growing children never has leftovers, so they had to look elsewhere to find scraps. Restaurants put a lot of good edibles on the curb in their waste cans and this is where Frank would head every morning with a bucket. The pig ate well due to these efforts, and on occasion Frank would find something he would take for himself. But the pig didn't know. The time comes for a pig when he is no longer the family guest but is invited into the house and the process is reversed.

Because of James Selvy's industry and his own athletic gifts, Frank was spared a life in the mines. Child labor in the mines had been abolished by the time he came along, but at age 12 he still made a significant contribution to the family income by picking tomatoes. He went to Indiana in the summer of that year as a migratory farm worker, earning 20 cents a basket. He found himself with pocket money for the first time, and even after sending half his earnings home to his mother he was able to enhance his social standing by buying a bicycle, a pair of basketball shoes and a tweed suit. He had the good judgement to buy a suit several sizes too big, though he really had no place to wear it. The basketball shoes were put to good use on the court of the Corbin YMCA.

These young boys developed their skills on the outdoor court at the Corbin YMCA and represented their town well in area competitions. Frank Selvy wears number 12 and is the second player from the left on the back row

As the summers progressed, Frank set higher goals for himself, eventually picking 100 baskets of tomatoes a day and earning $20 for his daily labor. It is one of the few accomplishments he talks about. The new status of a wage earner who had new shoes, a bicycle and a tweed suit led to other ventures, and in Kentucky a successful businessman goes to the horses. On a scale not so large but equally as risky, Frank and some of his pals pitched in $1.25 each and bought a horse. When people go into the horse business they learn that financial misfortune comes quickly to the naïve and uninitiated, and before any of them could take a ride, the great steed joined his ancestors. Poorer but wiser, the investors turned back to their bicycles, which provided more reliable transportation than a wobbly old horse one day away from the dog food can.

The Saturday picture show was a big thing in the lives of the boys and Frank earned 25 cents for cleaning up at a boarding house, which was the cost of admission. The strategy called for Frank to pay his way in and unlock the back door where his brothers and pals could join him. This worked well until the price of admission went up and the boarding house lady refused to raise his pay, so the new strategy was put into practice whereby they learned to open the back door from the outside.

No longer in the horse business and with the picture show problem solved, the boys turned their attention to other things, such as entering the county horse shoe competition...they had shoes salvaged from their investment.

4

Pitching Shoes and Shooting Hoops

It was every Kentucky boy's dream to put on the dark blue uniform of the Kentucky Wildcats and play for Adolph Rupp, the legendary basketball coach at the University of Kentucky. Rupp, too, was a poor Kentucky boy, whose mother had fashioned his first basketball using a gunnysack stuffed with rags. He became a star high school and college basketball player and had gone to helm the team at Kentucky two years before Frank was born. Rupp was known as "The Baron of the Bluegrass" and "The Man in the Brown Suit."

Frank and some friends began their basketball training by fashioning a crudely constructed goal on the side of a steep hill using anything they could find that was round and could bounce. Frank has often said that one of the reasons he developed his focus and shooting skills was because a missed shot meant the shooter had to chase the ball to the bottom of the hill. We all need incentives and we profit from the cost of making mistakes.

The YMCA was running—not walking—distance from the Selvy home. It had an indoor basketball court that was available in the winter and in bad weather, but the boys mostly honed their skills at the outdoor court. They played one-on-one or two-on-two using one basket, or full court using both. It was skins-and-shirts-no-blood-no-foul basketball. There were no referees with striped shirts and whistles and if you called touch fouls, you lost your status and even your right to play. Dribbling and ball handling, passing and shooting were the skills they honed, with toughness and tenacity the byproducts, along with a growing love of the game and of competition.

It's natural for boys to develop this love of a game and a desire to be good. It goes a step further when a boy feels a need to be the best and to seek perfection. To this boy, it goes beyond a mere game and becomes a contest where he despises making a bad play or taking a bad shot. This boy was Frank Selvy. But his love of the game wasn't limited to basketball.

On the yard at the YMCA alongside the basketball court, there were two horseshoe pits. Rural folks know this game and play it regularly. In a railroad town that brings in a lot of men from out of town living in boarding houses and hotels, they all played the game. It's easy to set up a pit because all you need are two iron stakes and two sets of horseshoes, which are always abundant wherever there are horses.

For the uninitiated, there are two styles of delivery. In one, the shoe is flipped end over end to the stake, but this causes the shoe to run and jump when it hits the ground the wrong way. The other style, preferred by more experienced players, involves tossing the shoe in a gliding motion that causes it to slide toward the stake, reducing the tendency to run and jump. Naturally, the good players use the glide-and-slide method. If you ring the stake you get five points, if you lean the shoe on the stake you get three, and if both players fall short, the one with the closest shoe to the stake claims one point. Horseshoes is not an easy skill to master but a dedicated player can excite the crowd by making it look easy.

At age 12, Frank entered the annual city-wide contest in Corbin. It's one of the few stories he tells on himself.

The contest offered two prizes, one for the singles winner and one for the doubles. Frank and one of his pals entered the doubles, which they won against the best players in town, including older and more seasoned players. The singles event followed, and it came down to a contest between Frank and his doubles partner. Frank tossed seven ringers in a row to win. That is comparable to shooting seven three-pointers in a row in a contested basketball game; it's done, but not often. He had swept the championship, at age 12.

Whether shooting hoops, tossing shoes or picking tomatoes, Frank Selvy was determined to excel. Soon he would prove himself on the court of his high school basketball team—even though he got a late start every season because he was still picking tomatoes when the other kids went back to the classroom.

5

Leaving Corbin

Despite the fact that Frank played only a season and a half at Corbin High School, in 1950 following his senior year, he was selected to play in a series of All-Star games in Indiana, Ohio and Kentucky. By then he had visited Furman University and greatly impressed Coach Bell with his shooting skills, but he still had the dream of all Kentucky boys of playing for Coach Rupp at the University of Kentucky. The All-Star games would be the place to catch his eye and land that basketball scholarship he wanted so badly.

The team members trained for a few weeks at Western Kentucky University and then traveled to Indiana for the first game. Frank sat out all but two minutes of that game and scored two points during his limited time on the court. It got better after that. In the final three games he started each time and was awarded the Most Valuable Player trophy. Conversations with Coach Rupp followed, but the Wildcat coach looked at the 150-pound six-footer from Corbin and decided Frank didn't have what it took to play in the paint. He was not tall enough or heavy enough to play center, he believed. It was one of the worst misjudgments of Rupp's coaching career. Frank got an offer from Western Kentucky, but somehow that fell through.

These events opened the door for a return to Furman University.

In 1950, Furman was a small liberal arts and sciences college affiliated with the Southern Baptist Convention. There were two campuses located several miles apart, one of which was originally Greenville Women's College. The other, formerly Furman Academy, was located in downtown Greenville beside the Reedy River. These schools combined during the Great Depression and busses ran between the campuses to accommodate class attendance and school activities. However, the women lived in dormitories under pretty strict supervision and the men at the downtown campus with little supervision other than the expectation of high moral conduct and the knowledge that violators would be expelled. Few students had personal cars, so the boys walked the couple of miles up Main Street in order to meet the girls and were never heard to complain.

The old campus appealed to the young man from Kentucky. He liked the Carnegie Library and the old main building with the bell tower covered with ivy. He could walk to class and downtown. He particularly liked the location of the gym, where he could go at night and shoot baskets for hours. It was here that he continued to perfect his revolutionary jump shot, which would be the ultimate complement to his ambidextrous ball movement and defensive agility. It would be a major contribution to basketball, adding the vertical dimension to the horizontal game.

Most Furman students were from South Carolina and adjoining states, with a sprinkling from other states and even foreign countries. Highly accredited, Furman also stressed high moral standards and good citizenship. Eventually, the university produced Dr. Charles Townes, who earned a Nobel Prize for his work on the laser, and many distinguished business, professional and political leaders, including a Rhodes Scholar. Frank would become Furman's first All-American basketball player and place its name on a marquee in bright lights in New York City.

Lyles Alley had become head basketball coach in 1945, leading the school to an impressive record in the old Southern Conference, the predecessor of the Atlantic Coast Conference. Furman's record in the state was very good and the Purple Paladins had won the respect of powerhouse teams such as Clemson, Duke, North Carolina, Maryland and North Carolina State. Furman's success came from the talented players produced by the local textile mill communities, whose recreational programs fed the teams at Parker High School and Greenville High School. It was an ideal operation for a low-budget program that relied on boys who lived at home and attended Furman as day students.

When Frank finally met Coach Alley, the coach was just as impressed with his skills as Interim Coach Bell had been.

"He told me that I could be All-American," Frank recalls. "He said that I could use my talents better here than anywhere else. Everything he promised me he delivered on. I know that I could not have accomplished the things that I did anywhere else—Kentucky or any other school. I would have played in a restricted role position under other systems, and at Furman I had a free range and open court to move in."

He accepted Coach Alley's offer and came to Greenville that summer, serving as a counselor at the mountain camp of Coach Red Dobson, who taught physical education at Furman and assisted with all the athletic programs. He had no reason to regret his decision, and remembers with pleasure being in charge of the camp's outdoor basketball court and its activities. Here he could do what he liked best...shoot baskets and put marks on the backboard to measure how high he could jump over the net and to provide an on-going challenge to move the mark higher.

The food was good and Coach Dobson was a gentleman of the highest order. The 17-year-old did what teens usually do in such an environment: he grew two inches and put on 30 pounds. The coaching staff at Furman didn't want that bit of information to get back to Lexington, Kentucky, so the remote camp provided another benefit...a place to hide the new asset Coach Rupp had let get away.

6

Coach Lyles Alley

Coaches need good players and they don't win many games without them. Good players also need good coaching and don't rise to the top without the teaching of a good head man. What else do they need? People who understand the game can answer this: teammates, loyal fans, support from the school and faculty…the list can be extended, but Furman University provided all this supporting cast behind Frank Selvy and his teammates during his four years as a Purple Paladin.

The centerpiece was Coach Alley. He made promises to the young prospect from Corbin, including the promise that he could become an All-American. How could Alley say that when he had never had an All-American on his team before? He might not have had an All-American, but he had coached many excellent players and the textile leagues in surrounding Greenville had many former All-Americans in their lineups. Coach Alley knew talent when he saw it and knew how to develop a talented player to the top of his ability.

The fact that Selvy was only six feet tall and weighed just 150 pounds didn't deter Alley from going all out to get the prospect, maybe because the coach was only five feet six inches himself but had earned 12 letters at Furman. (A man of five feet six has to look up to a man of six feet, so Selvy didn't look too small to him.)

Furman was in the Southern Conference, the best, and had played regularly against teams with national reputations. To be All-American, a player needs a lot of press coverage to provide the necessary exposure, and the coach told the coal miner's son that he would get it in the Southern Conference. The coach said it and Frank believed it and it happened.

They had a lot in common.

Jesse Lyles Alley was born in 1908 in Spartanburg, South Carolina. He spent his early years on a dairy farm sharecropped by his father and uncles. After his grandfather was injured in a mule wagon accident, the family moved into town, where young Lyles helped support his family by selling newspapers in the street. He and his childhood friend Gordon Blackwell built a basketball goal together and learned to shoot, sometimes playing at night to the light of a 10-watt bulb. When Alley graduated from Spartanburg High School, the Blackwell family helped gather funds to support him so he could accept an athletic scholarship at Furman.

Late summer night practices coupled with natural athletic ability led Alley to become a star college athlete. He graduated from Furman in 1933 as a four-year letterman in track, baseball, football and basketball. After graduating, he coached the Southern Bleachery textile league basketball team and the undefeated Miami, Florida senior high school football team in 1942. He served his country in the Navy during World War II, returning to his alma mater in 1945 as a coach. Over a 33-year career, Alley would serve as assistant football coach, head basketball coach, faculty member in the physical education department and university athletic director. In total, he supervised 20 seasons of basketball, retiring from coaching in 1966 as the university's most successful coach.

By that time, Coach Lyles had overseen 245 victories. His childhood friend Gordon Blackwell became the university's president in 1965.

Coach Alley was able to see the quality in his recruit, in part because they had followed the same road: building your own basketball goal and scrounging around for a ball, practicing long hours into the night, learning to scratch and scramble to get possession of the ball and to keep possession without committing a turnover. The best players learn this way and some of them do this while helping support their families, working long hours after school and still finding time to practice.

Lyles Alley had this love of the game and recognized it in his recruit, but they were both quiet about their private lives. Those who knew Alley best described him as a man who suppressed his emotions and had a coaching style that was tough and inflexible. He apparently felt it was necessary to keep his players humble, so he put a lot of emphasis on reminding them of their shortcomings and was very sparing with his praise.

Frank relates an incident that casts a lot of light on their relationship. Coach Alley taught the course in physical education that most of the Furman athletes took in their pursuit of a career in coaching. Selvy was a good student and wanted to really impress his coach with an assignment he was given to write a paper.

"I worked harder on that paper than any I had ever done," he recalled, "and spent a lot of time in the library doing statistical research in support of my conclusions. I knew it was good and when I turned it in I fully expected a good grade and praise from the head man. When he called me in, he told me that it was the best paper anyone had ever done in his class. So much for the praise because he then told me that I deserved an 'A' grade but he was only going to give me a 'C' because people would think that he was favoring me over the others."

Alley obviously found it necessary to deflate the grade because of what others would think. This was unfair, of course, but it was just one incident among many designed to keep his players humble. This is where it's necessary to view events in the light of the man's tough background and the things that made him the way he was. You can never go back home, but you never really leave…you take it with you.

According to some of Frank's teammates, this tough man also gave Selvy a little money to buy some suitable clothes upon his arrival at Furman. He had long outgrown the tweed suit he bought from picking tomatoes and had handed it down to his younger brothers. Alley reminded him that he was representing Furman and needed to dress the part. A week later the coach called him back into the office and proceeded to lecture him strongly because he was wearing the same old clothes. Reluctantly, an embarrassed   Selvy admitted he had sent the money home to his mother.

These are teaching moments, but the question arises as to who is the teacher. Frank had probably changed the tough little coach, rather than the other way around, but it's one of those stories "they say" that Selvy will not discuss.

7

Mentors and Role Models

There has been a lot said about the strategy employed by Coach Lyles Alley after walking away from Kentucky with the Most Valuable Player on its All-Star team. He knew that Adolph Rupp would quickly recognize the mistake of not signing Frank when he could. The All-Star games put the spotlight on the six-foot pivot man. Lyles Alley was there and made his pitch before any of the other coaches, and by the time they realized their mistake Alley had taken his prize to Miami for two weeks where he visited friends. He brought him to Greenville, and when a group of Kentucky supporters came to bring their native product home, he was not around... he was at Camp Pinnacle under the supervision of Coach Red Dobson.

Frank was put in charge of the basketball court and of teaching the younger boys the

"Red Dobson was a little bit of what every boy wanted to be when he grew up, and a lot of what grown men wished they had become."

fundamentals of the game as well as its fine points. One of his former charges recently recalled Frank hoisting him on his shoulders and having him make a mark on the backboard that would then become a new target for Frank to jump to…and then exceed. It has been said that "when one teaches, two learn."

It was widely applauded that Coach Alley had hidden his "asset" so that he couldn't be persuaded to come back home to the school he had always hoped to attend. The reader is called on to reconsider this appraisal of this strategy…perhaps he wasn't being hidden as much as he was being exposed to one of the most outstanding personalities in Furman athletic history. Lyles Alley was the only one to know the answer to this and he always kept his thoughts to himself unless he had a reason to express them, such as when dressing down a player he thought was under-performing, and there was never any room for misunderstanding when that occurred. Probably Lyles had both in mind and sent Frank to a place where he would be isolated but in the presence of a man who he would respect his entire life.

Frank has stated emphatically that the reason he didn't accept the new offer to play for Kentucky was because he had given his word to Alley and Furman. Those who know Selvy have no trouble believing this is true. Frank's wife, Barbara, says that if you don't want to hear the truth, don't ask Frank the question, because that is what you will get whether or not you like it. "Frank is frank," she says. The values instilled by his Bible-reading mother remain, and these values were reinforced by the examples and teaching of Coach Dobson.

Who was Red Dobson? What was his relationship to Coach Alley and Furman? The reader should know, and the best account of the life and career of the red-haired coach is an article by Ronald

Hyatt, a graduate of Furman and classmate of Selvy's. Titled "The Measure of a Man," it is appropriately on file in the archives of Furman University and provides the information for this chapter.

"Red Dobson was a little bit of what every boy wanted to be when he grew up, and a lot of what grown men wished they had become." This is how he is described by Hyatt, who worked as Dobson's assistant while a student at Furman and retained his admiration and respect for his mentor throughout his professional life. Frank Selvy echoes this sentiment when he discusses the man who welcomed him to his youth camp and immediately applied the force of his character to the Furman "asset" while providing him with one of the most enjoyable experiences of his life. It was a good time for the influence of a man with strong fundamental beliefs whose life reflected them.

Hubert Ray Dobson was born in Duplin County, North Carolina. His father died in a fall and the family moved to Wilmington, where his mother opened a boarding house. Wilmington was a railroad, logging, shipyard and seaport town on the Cape Fear River, and provided plenty of hard work for the strong, athletic young man. He entered Carolina Military Academy near Hendersonville in 1919, where he played football and other sports, and was offered a scholarship to Furman. He became one of the school's greatest athletes, lettering in four sports. Coach A.P. "Dizzy" McLeod recalled that Red was "a clean as well as hard-hitting player. A fine Christian young man who never cursed on or off the field, he was a fine influence for clean play and always had a good word for the other players." Lyles Alley knew him well and had every reason to entrust the development of his star player to him, with the knowledge that Frank would profit from the experience.

Dobson served as athletic director, intramural director and instructor in physical education. He enjoyed the love and admiration of the students at Furman, and during the summers he expanded his base of admirers with the young campers. He enjoyed his work and his colleagues, and all was right in the world until early in 1959, when he began to experience severe headaches and miss classes. On March 25, 1959, Red Dobson died of a brain tumor. He was 58 years old. It was a terrible loss for people from many places across America.

His strength and character are clearly reflected in the following paragraphs from Hyatt's article:

"Furman was then and still is a small college and at that time had just a little over a thousand students, which led to close identification with the faculty and each other. There was not a student at Furman who hadn't looked into his face and most of them had personal experiences with him through participation in physical education and sports.

"Red graduated from Furman in 1925 when he was All-Southern Conference in football and had lettered in four sports. He taught and coached at Spartanburg High School where his teams lost only five home games in 19 years and had undefeated seasons four times. His basketball teams won six state championships. Needless to say, they hated to see him go and he was named Spartanburg's most valuable citizen."

Hyatt quotes a Furman contemporary, Bobby Morrow, a Southern Baptist minister who recalled that Dobson once stopped a Furman gym class when a boy uttered an oath while playing basketball. Morrow said, "Mr. Dobson blew the whistle, turned to me and said, 'Bobby, I don't believe that boy said that, do you? He is too good a young man to say that. I don't believe he said it.' Then he gave us a 15-minute address on clean speech."

Another story Hyatt related was from Dobson's days at Spartanburg High School. During a faculty meeting, the subject of improper grammar came up. An English instructor suggested that "in every school activity, good English should be emphasized." Dobson stood, cleared his throat and said, "I have too much trouble in the gym keeping them from saying 'damn' and 'hell' to worry about them saying 'ain't' and 'nary.'"

Hyatt goes on to tell about the coach and his dog. Rex was a bulldog and was privileged to ride in the front seat of Red's Buick, while the assistant managers, including Hyatt, would ride in the back. One of the staff laughed and told Hyatt, using his nickname, "Hunkie, unless that dog dies, you're never going to get to ride in the front seat." Many people grade a man by how he treats his dog.

Red didn't worry about "ain't" and "nary," but he made it very clear that clean living and a high moral code were paramount in his life, and he expected the same from those over whom he had influence. Of course Lyles Alley had this in mind when he sent Frank to Camp Pinnacle.

When Coach Dobson died, a 200-car funeral caravan proceeded down Main Street in Spartanburg, where friends lined the entire route in a display of affection and respect.

8

The President and His First Lady

There were other Furman representatives who influenced the students, and they came in close daily contact with each other on the small downtown campus. Faculty members such as Winston Babb and Gene Looper would sit with small groups and engage in regular conversations with them and instill in them values that enriched the academic training of the regular curriculum. They knew your name.

Heading it all up and setting the standards were Dr. John Laney Plyler and his lovely "first lady," the former Miss Beatrice Dennis of Moncks Corner, who had become his wife in 1932. They had three sons. The president of Furman was a dignified and friendly man who presented the perfect image for the university, while his wife, who

could often be seen playing basketball in the yard with their sons, presented the ideal image of what a family should be. Frank had a close personal relationship with the president and his family. His son, John Plyler Jr., became active with the basketball program and remains a strong supporter.

When Adolph Rupp's representatives from the University of Kentucky called the Plyler home trying to locate Frank, the phone was answered by their John Jr., then 16 years old. This is how he recalls it:

"It was my first knowledge of Frank Selvy. It was late afternoon during the summer of 1950. My parents were out of town and I was at home alone. I answered the phone and the calling party asked to speak with my father. I informed the caller that my father was not at home and that I was uncertain of his return. The caller identified himself as Harry Lancaster, a basketball coach for the University of Kentucky, and asked if I knew where Furman was keeping Frank Selvy, so I told Mr. Lancaster that I was unaware of that person. In general, I remember Mr. Lancaster as being very demanding and seeming not to believe me."

Sometimes it's good not to know the answer.

Dean Francis Bonner told the story of Dr. Plyler in an article titled "A Man and a School" which can be read in the Furman Archives. Dr. Bonner said, "to tell the story of either is to tell the story of both…for more than a quarter century, in a very real way, John Plyler has been Furman University and Furman University has been John Plyler."

John Laney Plyler was born January 12, 1894, about five miles from the present Furman campus. His father was a Furman alumnus and a Baptist minister and his mother had graduated from Greenville Female College. John Plyler was a versatile young man who graduated from high school at age 15 and received a liberal arts degree from Furman, graduating magna cum laude in 1913. Always a student body leader, he earned a reputation as a star basketball player and as a "brain." He coached a championship basketball team at Greenville High School.

World War I came and Plyler served 18 months in the Army, rising from the rank of private to lieutenant. Law became his chosen field and he received a law degree from Harvard University in 1921. He practiced law in Greenville and taught law at the short-lived Furman Law School until he was elected to serve as the Greenville County court judge. On December 15, 1938, the trustees of Furman University chose him to be president of the school, an offer he "just couldn't refuse."

It's necessary to have a plan, but it's also necessary for others to provide the ingredients of success. Furman University was the place where such opportunities were waiting for the talented Kentucky basketball player who, like President Plyler, was to bring honor and distinction to both himself and his school.

9

Campus Life at Furman University

Furman University was a comfortable and friendly place to be in the 1950s. It didn't take long to make friends and find your place in a small student body where people knew who you were and made you feel at home. This was true of everyone on campus, but especially true for a talented and courteous young man from Corbin, Kentucky who displayed such skill on the basketball court. Frank was academically talented as well, sharing a dorm room with a similarly gifted non-athlete student. While he wanted to be the best on the court, he also wanted the advantages that come to an educated man, and he approached his studies with much of the same dedication he applied to the game.

The alma mater at Furman begins with the line, "A mountain city is her home; a mountain river laves her feat." The location of the two campuses in the heart of downtown Greenville on the banks of the Reedy River gave its students high visibility and put them in a setting where they could form associations and friendships with non-Furman people. Some of these people were contemporaries and some were business people and merchants who were part of a long tradition of local support for "The University." It was convenient for students to walk everywhere they needed to go, and this was important at a time when few of them had cars.

The Southern Baptist Convention contributed financially to the

A player can practice eight days a week but if he doesn't have the physical equipment he had better limit his competition to one-on-one in the driveway. Frank Selvy had the physique but was able to separate himself from the crowd by virtue of his focus and determination which led him to the practice court for hours on end, not just repeating the conventional shots but creating his own shots and moves.

university, and also had a large influence on its curriculum and faculty selections. Every student was required to take a course in Bible and attend chapel services.

Because of these connections, Furman's fan base included a large number of people who had no other association with the university. They came out to the games played at Greenville's main arena, Textile Hall, even when the team was losing. There had not been many such seasons and Furman had been state champions many times...but the team had never done well on "Tobacco Road" in North Carolina where Duke, the University of North Carolina, and North Carolina State set the standards for the entire country.

That was the case for the varsity team in 1950, when conference rules prevented freshmen from playing and relegated Frank to the junior varsity. The varsity team, long on effort but short on players, won only four games that season. The junior varsity, with its dazzling new player from Corbin, had an undefeated season. Although he never expressed it, Frank had a few misgivings about his future at Furman in light of his upcoming role on a varsity team with such a shortage of support players. Lyles Alley would address this problem.

Roger Thompson was one of the players on the losing varsity team in 1950 and a future teammate of Frank Selvy's. He recalls of their initial meeting in the summer of 1950, "It took only two or three minutes to show me that he was an enormously gifted player destined for greatness." The season to follow fulfilled the promise. "The freshman game was played first and they packed the seats, followed by the main game featuring the varsity, which played in front of half-empty seats. The games began to draw more than Furman students because the people in Greenville supported Furman and they knew and enjoyed good basketball."

This was crucial because ticket sales were the main source of income for the athletic program.

Thanks to his summer at Coach Dobson's camp, Frank was a much larger and taller player, and the conference took notice of the undefeated JV team. Word went back to Kentucky that the once-skinny boy was setting records, and wily Coach Rupp once again set about recouping the shooting star he had let get away. It was too late. The teaching of Iva Selvy, along with reinforcement from the highly ethical Red Dobson, had their effect. A good man's word is his bond and Frank had given his word to Furman.

10

Most Improved Team

It was a new day for Coach Lyles Alley. He had never had to go on the recruiting trail because the Greenville players always came to him. Besides, he had a very restricted budget which would not allow the extravagances of a traveling coach. Thanks to the added income generated by the freshman team's ticket sales during its undefeated 1950 season, he had a little more funding for recruiting trips. He could now plan a team and recruit the necessary players to fill the spots. (It's important to note here that television had not appeared on the college basketball scene, bringing big money and other monumental changes—both good and bad—to the game.)

Coach Alley needed a big man in the middle and he found him in Hutchinson, Kansas where the National Junior College Championship was taking place. He recruited Nield Gordon, a six foot six junior college All-American playing for Wingate College. Gordon had led his Brunswick, Maryland high school team to a first appearance in a championship game and he was looking for a four-year college home.

People talk about the perfect storm when conditions come together to create the ultimate in power and destruction. The same observation can be made when circumstances bring people's dreams and ambitions together in an ideal way. Coach Alley, at the crossroads in his career, was looking for a way to bring a team to a national stage. Frank Selvy was looking for an arena to perfect his dazzling array of skills and play a complete game. Nield Gordon had already heard the roars that his play for high school and junior college teams had generated and was looking to his future. All three were professional-grade performers—Alley as a coach and Selvy and Gordon as players destined to be drafted into the pros. They would lead Furman to its first conference tournament game and national recognition.

The varsity team boasted three talented returning players: Roger Thompson, Bud Granger and Bobby Chambers. Thompson, a Navy veteran, had come south from Green Bay, Wisconsin and in the process became more Southern than grits and eggs. He brought maturity and experience to the scene, having played in the service and suffered the pain of Furman's 1950 losing season. Chambers, a Greenville native, was a quick and athletic player who could work the ball around as well as shoot it. Granger, another product of Greenville, was big and strong and could hold a spot under the basket and put the ball in the hole. He was a football player with movie star good looks, which would have helped fill the seats with young girls even if he hadn't had the other skills.

These five players quickly formed a friendship that has lasted all their lives, complete with lots of joking and teasing. When a reporter asked Nield why he went to junior college instead of straight to four-year college, Frank jumped in and replied that it was because Nield could not read or write. Not true, of course, for Nield was intelligent as well as athletically talented, but he could appreciate a good joke...even when it was on him.

Joining these five were Gordon's junior college teammate and best friend Everette Pigg, who was also six foot six; Frank's high school friend Sylvester Wright; and A.D. Bennett, Guy Possinger, Bob Poole, Bob Roberts, and Buck Gay. The entire squad stepped in at crucial times during games and also dogged and tested the five leading players during practice scrimmages.

"We started slowly that year until Coach Alley moved Frank from forward, where he was penned up and restricted, to guard where he could face the basket, use his speed and have the freedom his game needed," Thompson recalled. "We played a brutally tough schedule—University of North Carolina, North Carolina State, Clemson and South Carolina twice each, then Duke, Miami and some very good in-state teams. Frank Selvy and Nield Gordon turned the program around as we rolled to 21 wins and became eligible for the Southern Conference Tournament for the first time in Furman's history."

The season opener was against North Carolina State and Frank was playing forward. At the forward position he was hemmed in, which stifled his shooting, but he still played defense and enabled his teammates to pick up the scoring. He scored 7 points, Gordon scored 18 and Granger 13. The reader is invited to compare this loss of 53 to 89 to their next meeting in the Southern Conference when Furman almost pulled off an upset, losing by just 5 points.

The second game was against North Carolina, a perennial giant, and Frank was held to just 7 points again. Thompson pumped in 20 points with his uncanny accuracy and led the scoring.

At Frank's request, Coach Alley moved him to guard, and it was an instant success. The next game, against Newberry College, allowed him to maneuver and he scored 16 points while Chambers made 18 and Gordon 27. Pigg had 14 and Granger 10, and the new style was beginning to pay off, with Furman winning by a score of 97 to 48.

In the game against Davidson College, Gordon and Selvy each scored 24 points, with Granger adding 12, Chambers 9 and Possinger 8. "Frank was the ultimate teammate as he scored from inside, on the post, and outside with a silky smooth jump shot. He defended just as effectively, rebounded and he was an excellent passer," Thompson said. "No one realized how unselfish he was in finding others open and making it so easy for the rest of us."

Selvy began earning nicknames. "We called him 'Slick' or

Just as the poet A.E. Housman wrote, it was not an unusual sight following a Furman game to see Frank Selvy, left, and Nield Gordon being carried shoulder high from the floor. It was a time of great reward for the players and excitement for the fans.

'Snake' because of his acrobatic twisting drives to the basket," Thompson said. "He had such hang time that he appeared to be suspended by wires."

During the regular season Furman beat Duke's top-rated team on the road by a score of 73 to 72. Duke's team featured their All-American Dick Groat, who later played professional baseball and basketball for Pittsburgh.

In the final game of the year, in the Southern Conference Tournament, Furman fell to North Carolina State after both Frank and Nield were fouled out on calls Thompson describes as "questionable." He admitted, "Without our stars we were doomed." But before that happened, Selvy scored 27 points, Gordon 17 and ever-steady Granger 10. Furman lost 68 to 73, prompting this commentary from the *Charlotte Observer*:

> *Furman stirred a huge Southern Conference tournament crowd here last night by almost upsetting North Carolina State. The fact that they lost by five points does not diminish their deserved credit. They were able to make the monumental effort:*
>
> 1. *Because a kid from Corbin, Ky., named Frank Selvy, got tired of waiting for his State University to take some interest in him and at the invitation of a soft-spoken coach named Lyles Alley elected to follow two friends (a ministerial student and a football player) to a Baptist institution in South Carolina; because when a posse of Kentucky scouts came looking for him in Greenville, Frank had sanctuary at a summer camp in Hendersonville, North Carolina;*

2. *Because a big boy named Nield Gordon, who lives only three miles from the U. of Maryland campus, was not sufficiently mature to impress Terp coaches at the time he sought admission; because after two years of junior college at Wingate the exceptionally agile blond was ready to matriculate at Furman, where the same Lyles Alley continued the process begun by [Wingate Coach] Danny Miller;*

3. *Because a set shot marksman named Roger (Swede) Thompson, who had a schedule of 400 practice shots daily, was able to make four straight against State and then had the intense feeling to break into tears and blame himself when he missed a fifth one that might have given Furman the ball game.*

4. *Because of such operatives as A.D. Bennett of Holly Hill, South Carolina, who with the fresh confidence of the young failed to understand that his team was sure to be beaten badly; because of a coltish camaraderie that would move the entire club to peroxide their hair on last December's trip [to the Orange Bowl] to Florida—because that all-for-one feeling was a big factor in their becoming the Conference's basketball golden boys."*

The writer went on to say that he intended to place the name of Lyles Alley on his ballot for Conference Coach of the Year.

The incredible turnaround won Furman recognition as "Most Improved" team in the nation for the 1951-52 season. The prestigious award was presented by the U.S. Rubber Company, based on

Decked out in new suits provided by an anonymous Greenville fan are members of the 1951-1952 Furman basketball team. On the left side of the table, front to back, are Frank Selvy, Roger Thompson, Bob Poole, Bud Granger, Nield Gordon and Coach Melvin Bell. At the head of the table is Coach Lyles Alley. On the right side from front to back are Bobbie Roberts, Bobbie Chambers, Buck Gay, Everett Pigg, Guy Possinger, Joe Small and A.D. Bennett. The team was enjoying their trip to New York and their appearance in Madison Square Garden.

national rating systems. The other players worked well with their stars and took pride in the fact that no other team in history had risen from the bottom to such prominence as Furman did that year. "Furman was proud, we were proud, and to show how much Greenville loves Furman, an anonymous businessman bought us all suits for the trip to Raleigh and the tournament," Thompson said. "It was the first and only suit some of us had."

Here are some of the National Collegiate Athletic Bureau statistics for Furman at the end of the 1951-52 season:

- Frank Selvy ranked 5th among the nation's top scorers with an average of 24.6 points per game

- Nield Gordon ranked 18th with an average of 20.5 points per game

- Selvy placed 2nd in single game scoring leaders. He scored 49 points against Wofford College, just one less than Bob Petit of Louisiana State University, the No. 1 single game scorer. Selvy placed 12th in the same rankings with his 44-point night against Virginia Military Institute.

- In single game free throws, Selvy ranked 11th with 14 of 18 attempts against Wofford.

- Furman ranked 13th in the nation for team offense, with an average of 75 points per game.

- Furman ranked 6th in the nation in field goal percentages, hitting the hoop 39.2 percent of the time.

- Furman ranked 16th in the nation for the fewest personal fouls committed per game, with an average of 19.8.

In addition to those statistics, here are a few more facts:

- Furman reached the Southern Conference tournament for the first time. The game with North Caroline State was described as one of the best of the tournament.

- Selvy was named to the Converse Rubber Company third All-American team and to the All-Southern Conference team, and Gordon was named to the second All-Conference team, despite their having played in only one game in the tournament.

- Both Selvy and Gordon received honorable mentions on numerous all-star and All-American selections.

There would be many more accolades to come.

Looking back on the 1951-52 season, it is obvious why the Paladins created such a stir in Greenville and all over South Carolina. Basketball was taking a step up from being "the other sport" to its place as a top attraction in the sports world. There would be full scholarships for basketball players and the days of total reliance on football players and athletes from other sports were ending. The game evolved, and those who played it well brought changes to the way it was played. The fan base grew.

11

The Outstanding 1952-53 Team

The Paladins entered the 1952-53 season with its central five intact, though there were concerns about an eye injury Bobby Chambers had suffered and how it would impact his game. Preseason discussions centered not only on the winning duo of Selvy and Gordon but on the improved playing of A.D. Bennett and the steadiness and reliability of Bud Granger at guard. Roger Thompson had graduated and was headed to Korea with the Army. Guy Possinger and Bob Poole, both reserves, had not returned to school.

Coach Alley knew the Most Improved Team still had a way to go and had brought in new talent to take them there. These promising newcomers included Ken Deardorff from Gettysburg, Pennsylvania, a junior college transfer who was a sharpshooter from the outside and a smooth ball handler. He was needed to bring the ball up court. Fred Fraley had come in from Wayland, Kentucky, and six foot six player Bob Thomas hailed from Miami. The roster also added Nield Gordon's brother, Brock, who was big and strong.

The season got off to a poor start for Furman by losing to North Carolina State—their nemesis from the previous season—as well as Mercer and Davidson colleges. They then defeated Richmond College by two points, launching a turnaround. They came within a whisker of defeating Manhattan College in their first appearance in Madison Square Garden. Then they won the next eight straight games before losing to South Carolina (Selvy was injured and on the bench.) That loss was followed by 12 wins in a row. The Paladins never lost a game in their home court of Textile Hall and got revenge for all of their defeats except North Carolina State and West Virginia, having played these teams only once.

The 1952-53 Paladin squad astounded the fans once again when they won 21 of 27 games and continued to rewrite the record book. Frank was the leading scorer in the nation, racking up 738 points in the season, and was also the greatest per game performer among major colleges with an average of 29.3 points per game. In the game against Mercer College, Frank scored 63 points, the highest single game score for the season among major colleges. It was the fourth highest single game total for a player in major college basketball history.

As a team, the Paladins scored over 100 points in nine games—another record—and the team's average of 90.1 points a game set a new college record in that era. Percentage-wise, they established another record by making 44.4 percent of field goal attempts.

The 73-74 loss to the Manhattan Jaspers was another first for Furman, as it was played on December 20, 1953 at the country's premier arena, Madison Square Garden. Furman's name was displayed in lights on the marquee in New York's Midtown, while the folks at home later watched the game on a downtown theater screen, television having not quite entered the scene. No one in Greenville had ever heard of a Jasper, unless they had an uncle by that name, and none of the fans in New York had heard of a Paladin, as the popular television show featuring a gunslinger by this name was several years away. They were well-matched teams from two sides of the Mason-Dixon Line.

Here are some quotes from the *New York Times* article by Joseph M. Sheehan:

Manhattan trips Furman 74 to 73 in Garden Battle

Manhattan had Cappy Lane to thank for its fourth straight basketball victory last night. Madison Square Garden's official timekeeper, to whom the decision was referred, ruled that what would have been a game-winning goal for Furman had been tallied after the final buzzer. So the undefeated Jaspers won 74 to 73.

Furman, which had lost three of four previous starts, was making its first appearance in New York, surprised everyone, including the Jaspers, in carrying the fight so strongly to a Manhattan team that is co-rated with Fordham as the best of the local quintets.

While Manhattan forced the play for most of the game, the Green never was able to shake off the stubborn pursuit of the Southern Conference five. The teams, deadlocked seven times in all, finished the half in a 41-all tie.

Manhattan spurted to a 64-56 lead in the third quarter and still was ahead by 9 points after two minutes of play in the final period. But the gallant South Carolinians promptly charged back to a 69-all tie.

A shot by Gerry Cahill put the Jaspers ahead with five minutes to go. Tom Hunt added a foul, but Ken Deardorff, high scorer for Furman with 21 points, pumped in a one-hander to leave the Paladins only a point behind.

Just before the three-minute mark, when the two-shot

foul rule went into effect, Willard Doran sank a foul to give a 73-71 edge and the Jaspers went into a "freeze." When it appeared as if the Jaspers had run out the clock successfully, Fred Fraley and Frank Selvy swooped down on Hunt, who was backed against the restraining line. Fraley knocked the ball loose from the Manhattan player's hand, and almost in the same motion flipped it to Selvy, who was racing for the basket. Furman's fleet forward scooped up the ball, poised himself and let fly. His shot banked cleanly through the hoop.

The final buzzer sounded and the end-of-game red light flashed almost simultaneously with Selvy's shot, so Referee Hagan Andersen, after signaling that the shot had gone in, turned inquiringly to Lane.

Cappy gave the "too-late" sign and that was the last word of as stirring a basketball game finish as the Garden had ever seen. In the scoring column: Selvy had 15, Granger 17, Fraley 2, Gordon 12, Deardorff 21, and Chambers 6.

There were no replay cameras at that time so the timekeeper's call was final. When the game was shown in the theater in Greenville, the highly partisan Furman fans booed mightily when the disputed call appeared on the screen.

A team can take pride in its accomplishment even in a loss, and the Paladins and their fans did.

12

Senior Season

At the end of the 1952-53 season, Frank's classmates at Furman conferred another honor upon him, electing him senior class president. This recognized that Frank was an all-around student who had excelled on the court while taking advantage of the educational opportunities offered by Furman and making lifelong friendships. He took the difficult courses and excelled in them, winning membership in prestigious honor societies that recognized the best on campus.

Walter B. "Blackie" Cook, a classmate, fellow member of the Blue Key and Quaternion Club, and former vice president and board member of Quaker State Corporation, has this to say:

"Frank's qualities and character off the basketball court were also recognized by his classmates and Furman's administration. He was a member of the Quaternion Club, Furman's oldest and most exclusive society. It was established in 1903 to recognize student leadership. Only a few students are selected each year from the junior and senior classes. A number of Furman's presidents have been members. He was also a member of Blue Key, an honorary fraternity with members selected on the basis of their campus activities and general record of achievement."

The student newspaper, *The Hornet*, named him Student of the Year for 1953, recognizing him as the student who had "made the largest contribution toward the fame and fortune of Furman University during the past year. Smashing one basketball record after another, he has literally 'put Furman on the map.'"

Continued *The Hornet*, "It was Selvy who scored 1,328 points during his first two seasons for an all-time high of any varsity man in the nation in his first two years...But it is not for these honors alone that *The Hornet* salutes Frank Selvy. His spirits of humbleness and humility, of cooperation and capability, have made him a man to respect and remember on the Furman campus."

Another accolade followed. The leading newspaper in his home state, the *Louisville Courier-Journal*, named him Kentucky Athlete of the Year. His nicknames now included "Fabulous Frank" and "The Corbin Comet."

This would be the last year of the Selvy era. The now All-American and leading scorer in the nation had proven himself in so many ways, and Furman had come such a long way, the question once again was "Where do we go from here?" A coach's first step in devising a strategy is to evaluate the players and their strengths and weaknesses. Lyles Alley knew he had shooters and ball handlers. The addition of Darryl Floyd had given him added dimension in those areas, but he knew the same thing his opposing coaches knew: the middle was the major concern. Nield Gordon was gone and he would be missed.

Brock Gordon, Nield's younger brother, had these things to say about the situation:

"It was my impression that Coach Alley was expecting that Furman would not be as strong as in the previous season for two reasons. One was that opposing teams would be a little better prepared to defend against Frank, who they knew could score whether driving, shooting the jump shot or playing the pivot. Second, Furman had lost Nield, a strong inside player who would be difficult to replace. His answer was to expose his team to a challenging preseason."

The Greenville area was still home to a number of amateur/semi-pro basketball teams composed of highly skilled players from colleges or local mills. They were hired by the textile companies to instill pride in their workers and for the entertainment of the community. Alley had his team play at least five of these, both to give them experience and to enable him to see what they had. Dunean Mill featured two players from Indiana University, which had won the NCAA Championship the previous year. Enka Mills had a seven-footer from Wofford College, "Big Daddy" Neal, who later joined the Syracuse Nationals of the NBA.

The Paladins also traveled to Parris Island, South Carolina to face a strong all-star Marine team, which included Paul Arizin and Richie Guerin. Arizin had graduated from Villanova in 1950 after leading the nation in scoring and becoming a three-time consensus All-American. He played with the Philadelphia Warriors for one season and led the NBA in scoring before serving the next two years in the Marine Corps. (He returned to the Warriors for eight years after that.) Guerin was drafted by the New York Knicks in 1954, where he became a leading scorer and six-time All-Star pro player. As a player and coach he was elected to the Naismith Hall of Fame.

In addition to these almost professional teams, Alley scheduled practice games against highly competitive college teams, including the University of Miami, Tulane and Louisiana State University, all on their home courts. LSU was a high-powered team in 1953 and

FRANK SELVY, Furman's All-Southern and honorable mention All-American, crams a full schedule into his daily campus routine. After early morning classes, Frank is shown above as he strolls down the steps of the library. Like most

Selvy came to Furman University to play basketball—and get an education. Shown leaving the library on a typical day, Selvy was an honor student and also elected student body president in his senior year.

became champions of the Southeastern Conference that year. Its star player was Bob Petit, a two-time All-American. By the time the season opened, the wily little coach knew very well what his team's strengths and weaknesses were.

The 1953-54 schedule was distinctly different. The Atlantic Coast Conference had been formed, taking the eight major teams out of the Southern Conference. Even so, Furman was still the opponent for the North Carolina State opening game, played as usual on the State home court in Raleigh. With the loss of Gordon, State exploited the weak middle and won easily.

Furman lost six of its first seven games, but the team persevered and the skills of Darrell Floyd and the returning Ken Deardorff, plus the improvement of sophomore center Bob Thomas, began to pay dividends. Furman won 20 games, including an upset rematch against the Jaspers in Madison Square Garden. Selvy gained national and permanent fame by shooting 100 points in one game—to be covered in the next chapter—and was named Outstanding Player of the Nation by United Press International sportswriters. He scored 50 or more points eight times during the season.

In the Southern Conference tournament in Morgantown, West Virginia, the Paladins beat Davidson College 84-68 in their first game and lost to Richmond College 85-81 in an overtime thriller. Selvy was elected to the All-Tournament team and was No. 1 in the balloting. Darrell Floyd, who was to become Furman's next All-American, was selected to the second team. He was the nation's seventh leading scorer, with an average of 25 points per game, and joined Selvy in becoming the highest scoring duo in the nation. (Selvy had previously shared that honor with Nield Gordon.)

Once again, Furman University found itself in the spotlight and the legend of the coal miner's son grew. In particular, the sophisticated patrons of Madison Square Garden had their memories refreshed when the Paladins returned for their second meeting with the Jaspers on February 4, 1954.

Frank was sent ahead of the team to a New York armory, where he worked out alone. Well, not totally alone, because the press corps was there popping photos as he launched jump shots. It was one of the tests all players face after being built up in the press: they need to repeat the performances which brought them the attention in the first place. It didn't take the reporters long to learn Frank didn't have a lot to say. Instead, he spoke through his performances.

Frank was quietly eloquent when Furman took the floor in the Garden. The seats were filled with fans who remembered the most exciting game of the previous season when the timekeeper's ruling denied Furman its winning basket. This is how *Greenville News* Sports Editor Jim Anderson told the story:

Fabulous One Snaps Garden Point Record

New York, Feb. 4, 1954—Fabulous Frank Selvy showed 6,639 in Madison Square Garden here tonight he is an All-American as he was sensational in scoring 42 points to set a new 1953-54 Garden scoring record and pace the Purple Paladins to a 92-80 upset victory of the Manhattan Jaspers. Selvy smashed an all-time Garden record in making 16 free throws good. He was helped in this by brilliant ball handling to keep possession in the closing minutes when green-shirted Jaspers fouled him in their desperation.

Selvy broke a Garden record of 36 points held this season by Richie Guerin of Iowa, and the Paladins rolled up the most points ever scored against a Manhattan team. In the first half the partisan crowd was chanting at Selvy, "Watch the average." Frank didn't have to watch anything but the basket and he found it was there. He hit 13 field goals in 27 attempts and 16 free throws in 16 attempts. He also got 10 rebounds.

Manhattan had the first goal of the game and went off to an early lead as though the Jaspers would be every bit the 10-point difference they were favored. They went to 15-6 before the Purples could start closing the lead. [Darrell] Floyd hit for two beautiful field goals to slash the Jasper lead 15-13. Selvy had his first point of the game on Furman's 14th point, when he made good on free throws. [Fred] Fraley and [Ken] Deardorff banged in field goals and Furman led for the first time 18-17. Manhattan went back to a 20-18 lead and then Selvy started hitting. Frank quickly made it a 20-all. With the first quarter running out, the Purples turned red hot. They ran to score to 27-20 as the first quarter ended.

Floyd and Selvy shot field goals and Fraley had two free throws to put it at 36-20. Furman had scored 18 points while holding Manhattan scoreless. Furman led 57-44 at halftime. Furman kept the lead and won the game 92-80. It was a big night for Furman and a bigger one for Selvy.

This type play had been repeated many times during the 1953-54 season in places like Philadelphia against LaSalle before a record-breaking crowd of 9,164. LaSalle's big six-foot-seven All-American center Tom Gola was the deciding factor in gaining his Explorers a 100-83 victory over the Paladins, but Frank out-scored him, 40 points to his 25.

The revenge at Madison Square Garden was a huge night in Frank's life. But the basketball game that made him a legend took place nine days later.

13

The 100-Point Game

There are people who always want to talk about the 100-point game whenever Frank Selvy's name comes up. Frank doesn't bring it up himself. To him it was something he did on February 13, 1954 when Furman University and Greenville set out to honor their hero by declaring Selvy Day and structuring the game in a manner that would showcase Frank in a match against a good Newberry College team.

In truth, he would rather talk about the record he set as a teenager picking tomatoes, when he picked 100 baskets in one day and earned a much-needed $20. But the record he set filling another kind of basket 100 times is what most people remember about his career, and it's impressive whether or not you are a sports fan—or a gourmet with a love of tomatoes.

Frank's parents, James and Iva, arrived in Greenville by train, while six siblings and many Corbin friends and neighbors traveled the 250 miles in a 22-car caravan.   At halftime, five of Frank's younger brothers, coached by sister Stella, played a game against a local team. Each of the Selvys wore a white shirt with their name on the front and Frank's jersey number 28 on the back.

It was the first basketball game—in fact the first athletic event—ever televised live in South Carolina. This was an introduction to a new era in the sport, the beginning of a transformation of college basketball. No longer would the teams be solely dependent on the revenue from gate receipts. Television networks with paid sponsors turned basketball into a profitable enterprise for both the media and the schools. Athletic shoe manufacturers and their representatives would give their products to the coaches for their players to wear, thereby promoting their products on the air. The fan base was greatly expanded and much more commodious facilities were built to accommodate them, thus increasing ticket sales. Larger and more colorful crowds appealed to the television audience and it all became more exciting and profitable.

James Selvy, the coal miner, his wife Iva and daughter Stella display serious faces on the evening of Frank Selvy Night at Textile Hall. They watched Frank set an all-time collegiate record by scoring 100 points in a Division 1 basketball game. It was only the second time that the miner had seen his son play: the previous time was two nights earlier when   Frank scored 51 points against Georgia Tech.

But in South Carolina, it all began on February 13, 1954.

Here's how Bob Gillespie, senior writer for *The State* newspaper, told it in a look-back interview with Frank published on February 8, 2004, fifty years after the fact:

That cold, rainy night was Frank Selvy night, and Furman Coach Lyles Alley, a consummate showman, had big plans... Television station WFBC produced the state's first live telecast of an athletic event. Alley even arranged for a seven-piece jazz band, including trombones and a washboard player, to perform at halftime.

And showing a sense of history, Alley had hired a cameraman to film the game from the stands—a rarity in those pre-video days, and a decision that would pay benefits to Furman 50 years later.

Then again, Alley didn't need a crystal ball to expect fireworks from Selvy. The senior forward had lit up scoreboards across the Southeast that season, scoring 50 or more points three times and 40-plus five times in earlier games. Two nights earlier, in a 114-67 rout of Georgia Tech, Selvy had gone for 51.

So why Newberry for Selvy's night? "It was sort of close to the end of my senior year," Selvy says, "and maybe (Alley) wanted to make sure I scored a lot and we won."

From the opening tip, Selvy made Alley's preparations look inspired. He drove for a layup, was fouled and made the free throw, less than five seconds from the tip. An auspicious start.

Newberry and Furman played racehorse that night, and Textile Hall's 82-foot court, three Selvy strides shy of regulation, didn't hurt the pace. The Indians' coach, Red Burnette, later admitted he'd thought about slowing things down, even holding the ball.

"But I said, What the heck? We're here to play," he said. "If (Selvy) could score a bundle, why not." Besides, in an earlier meeting, Furman struggled to beat Newberry, and Selvy scored only 23 points.

Not this time, though. College games then consisted of four 10-minute quarters, and after one, Selvy had 24 points. Newberry player Bobby Bailey fouled out in the first 2:43 trying to guard him, and replacement Sam Coleman was having no better luck.

Word spread around Greenville, and people left what they were doing to jam into Textile Hall. Bob Cole, now a retired sports writer for The State, *was part of a band, The Satins, who found their performance at a nearby hotel suddenly abandoned. Cole also ran to the game, but couldn't get close enough to the court to see anything. "The fire marshal would've closed the place down if he'd happened by," he says.*

By halftime, Furman led 77-44, and Selvy had 37 points while teammate Darrell Floyd, who would lead the nation in scoring the next two seasons, had 25. But this wasn't about pummeling the Indians. This was about Selvy. So Alley made two decisions. First, he ordered the team to change from its silver jerseys to purple so the cameraman's black and white film could more easily distinguish them from Newberry's white—a precursor to basketball's modern, TV-driven rules for uniforms.

And Alley told Floyd and the rest of his starters that they would sit the second half. The rest of the Hurricane players had one order: Feed Frank.

Resentment? Hardly. "I felt great about it," says Fred Fraley, the team's starting point guard. "We felt it was an opportunity for Frank to make All-American. We were struggling then to get recognition, even in South Carolina. We got a lot of it through that." Selvy also had no qualms. "Everybody had a role," he says. "A lot were happy just to be playing. Some couldn't score points." Guys like Joe Gilreath, a stocky ex-football tackle, who says, "Coach Alley sent me in as a wrecking crew if another team tried to rough up Frank."

This night, all Selvy needed was the ball. He made 41 of 66 goal attempts, hitting shots from everywhere, on all sorts of moves. Long rainbows that would be worth three points today. Sudden drives to the rim. Rebounds and put-backs. Plus, his patented low-post, spinning hook shots that Alley always said were Selvy's best weapon. "I was just so confident in my ability to play, and my relationship with Coach Alley," Selvy says. "I knew he wasn't going to take me out, no matter what happened."

In fact, Selvy played every minute of that 29-game season. Nield Gordon, who later coached at Newberry and Winthrop, had played his final season at Furman when Frank was a junior, but he was listening to the game on the radio. He remembered then what Jake Penland, sports editor of The

State, *once told Alley. He said, "'Coach, at Furman you need
to get as much publicity as you can, Frank needs to stay in as
much as he can,'" Gordon says. "Alley had heeded that advice."*

*After three quarters, Selvy had 63 points and Furman
led, 109-66. In the final period, with the public address
announcer shouting out a running total over the roar of the
crowd, Selvy scored 37 of Furman's 40 points. But he saved
the best moment for last.*

*"They threw the ball to me" with seconds left, Selvy says,
"and I got it near mid-court." Triple teamed, he took a couple of dribbles, turned and shot. "I did a spin move and sort
of let it go."*

*The 16mm film, now saved on videotape, shows a high
shot coming down, swishing through the net after the horn
sounds. Gilreath, on the bench then, says his image of that
shot is "as vivid now as the sun shining yesterday." Selvy
afterwards said he knew his 40-50 footer was good when it
left his hand. "It felt like it was in, yeah," he says now, smiling. Told that, Gilreath laughs. "If Frank says it felt good,"
he says, "he must've had a straight line to up above."*

Maybe, in fact, he'd had that all along.

Frank was presented with the game ball, but instead of enshrining it
in a glass case, he gave it to his younger brothers who wore it out on
the outdoor court of the YMCA in Corbin. They followed his example and became college basketball players.

What makes a man behave in such an unassuming manner?
Frank's teammate Bobby Chambers puts it well. "Frank is very quiet

in a crowd but is totally different when he's with his friends. He's very loyal and supportive of this group and very humorous. He is very modest and I have never heard him speak about his achievements or ambitions except that I know he wanted to build his mother a brick house and, with the help of his brothers, did it. He wanted to help his family and especially his younger brothers…He did this also. I would be an admirer and friend of Frank Selvy even if he had never seen a basketball, and this friendship has lasted more than 60 years. We still get together for golf and we still go to church services together."

Bobby and some of Frank's other teammates are part of a group of retired men, many from Furman but including every school Furman played, that get together on golf courses for regular games. They call themselves the Good Guys.

To many of the guys, a few good shots

Textile Hall, demolished in 1992, was the site of Textile Tournaments, with two games going simultaneously, as well as Furman basketball during the Selvy era. Pictured at a reunion in front of the building are, from left, Frank Selvy, Nield Gordon, Roger Thompson and Everette Pigg.

and an occasional birdie are sufficient to provide conversation in the coffee shop, but that is not true of Frank. All golfers hate to make a bad shot but find redemption in making a good shot later. They can turn the page and the bad shot is accepted and forgotten. Frank can't do that; he takes it home with him. Like every other sport he played, golf is a contest in which he strives for perfection and a bad shot drives him to the practice range and later to a golf book for the answer he needs. Where older golfers wonder about how wide and how long the fairways are and the quickness of the greens, Selvy wonders about the course record. He may not say it, but he wants it.

Besides basketball, he has won at horseshoes, darts, bowling, baseball, arm wrestling and even Indian wrestling. He has trophies to show for it—but they're in his basement, not on his mantel.

14

Fans

Heroes abound in the world of sports and entertainment and the enthusiastic fan base at Furman quickly expanded into Greenville, attracting an impressive variety of supporters. Fathers brought their sons and daughters to the games and these business and professional leaders joined in the chorus of such roars of approval as would rattle the windows of old Textile Hall as they had never been before. Standing room only crowds created serious concerns from the fire department and ticket sales thrilled the director of finance at the university. The Paladin team was honored wherever they went. When they ate out they would often be pleasantly surprised when they found that the check had been paid by an anonymous fan. The quiet young man from Kentucky was no longer able to blend into the crowd.

On March 2, 1954 the South Carolina Senate adopted the following resolution:

IN APPRECIATION OF FRANKLIN D. SELVY, A STUDENT OF FURMAN UNIVERSITY.

Be it resolved by the Senate of the State of South Carolina:

We note with pride the achievements of Franklin D. Selvy in attaining the status of All-American as a basketball player, and in holding the world's record in every known phase of scoring in basketball.

Not only is he outstanding in the field of Sports, but he is a young man of the very highest character. While he has been showered with praise and the plaudits of all who love clean sports, he remains modest, humble and unassuming. He furnishes the youth of this country who love clean sports and physical culture with an example that everyone would do well to emulate.

Not only is he a credit to his team, to the University in which he is a student, but he is a credit to the State of South Carolina.

Be it further resolved, that copies of this resolution be sent to Franklin D. Selvy, his coach, Mr. Lyles Alley, and to the president of Furman University, Dr. John L. Plyler.

Not to be outdone, the legislature of Kentucky named Frank a Kentucky Colonel, and he was presented the keys to the City of Corbin, which also named a street after him. When asked about the street Frank says that "it isn't very long but sufficiently wide."

When you conjure up a picture of a young basketball fan, you would naturally expect to see a young boy aspiring to play the game. There were many of these, but there were others. The following essay was lifted from the scrapbook of Nancy Smith, kept when she was a student at Anderson Girls High School. She composed it as a senior, looking back to her "impressionable youth." Over 60 years later, she is as amused as most people are when recalling their youth.

RAPTURE
By Nancy Smith

Yesterday I had a good laugh at myself. I was reminiscing about my youth, the days before I became a wise and mature senior, the days when I was subject to silly and absurd things—even crushes on much older men. The experience I was thinking about was my crush on a college basketball star.

For months I had admired that tall, dark-haired grand looking player. But even worse than that, I actually kept a scrapbook of every word that was written about him. My room was filled with 113 pictures of that fabulous face.

Since my father is an alumnus of that college, we seldom missed one of their games. On one of those nights my uncle went with us. To understand the rest of my story, you will have to understand my uncle. He is an extrovert in the truest sense of the word. Uncle Walter goes on the principle that when someone wants something, he should get it. So when he found out that my chief desire was to meet fabulous Frank Selvy, he calmly took me by the hand after the game, pushed his way through the crowd, and led me elegantly to him.

I just couldn't believe that he was actually smiling at me, shaking my hand, and politely replying "yes, of course" when my forward uncle matter-of-factly said, "you know Nancy."

All these things that happened one night four years ago were brought of mind while I was looking through my old scrapbook. For there on one page marked "IMPORTANT" was the glove, still unwashed, which he had held in his big, strong hand and the program with that wonderful, sprawling autograph. But most important of all was the large stain where he had actually perspired on my program!

He perfected it on the playground at the YMCA in Corbin. No one showed it to him and he had never been coached and yet he became the leading scorer in the country on this shot, which he introduced to the college game. Playing under the basket while shorter and lighter than the big boys he developed an additional skill…the jump shot with a lean backwards that made it almost impossible to block by even the tallest of the other players. If you want to perfect the jump shot, look at this picture of the man who invented it, taken in 1949, his first year at Furman.

They were not all boys and men…there were young girls who would go on to successful lives and who could still recall with nostalgia and amusement their involvement in the Frank Selvy period of Furman basketball. Sixty years later, Nancy is amused but not ashamed of her juvenile crush on a man so widely admired, and she isn't alone.

15

Drafted

The National Basketball Association was not near so big and powerful in 1954 when Frank was the No. 1 draft pick and was selected by the Baltimore Bullets at the then unheard of salary of $10,000 a year.

It was following the 1948-49 season that the NBA replaced the Basketball Association of America, which was always perched on the edge of financial disaster. An example of their precarious fiscal position is cited by Charley Rosen in his fine history of the NBA *The First Tipoff.* When the team owners were summoned to a meeting on June 6, 1947, they were advised to have lunch *before* the meeting, as the BAA could not afford to feed them.

Frank had led the nation in collegiate scoring two years in a row, was first pick All-American and had proved himself on the national scene, especially during the games at Madison Square Garden. After the second Manhattan game, Coach Red Auerbach of the Boston Celtics was waiting for Frank. Auerbach not only had an eye for a good cigar but was one of the best in the business at judging talent. He told Frank he liked the way he played and would love to draft him, but he knew that those with prior draft choices wouldn't let that happen.

The college draft system was initiated in the 1947-48 NBA season as another way to bring fresh college players into the professional level, thereby increasing the fan base and generating badly needed revenue. The professional teams had to compete with the well-paid and talented semi-professional teams fielded by companies such as Caterpillar and Phillips Petroleum. These corporate teams could guarantee players steady payment and a life-time career.

The only NBA team that contacted Frank in 1954 was the Baltimore Bullets, which had the first draft pick. He conferred with Coach Lyles Alley about what to expect in an offer. Alley thought Frank should hold out for $4,000 and suggested that they get local attorney Dick Foster, brother of *Greenville News* Sports Editor Dan Foster, to aid in the negotiations. Dick Foster was a good lawyer and Lyles Alley was a good coach but neither had any knowledge or experience that would have benefitted Frank. The Baltimore coach nixed that, but sent Frank the money to travel up for an interview.

Baltimore opened the discussion with an offer of $9,000. Frank was stunned speechless and after he had sat looking at the coach a minute, the offer was upped to $10,000. It was the highest ever made to a rookie. But it wasn't his only option. Both Caterpillar and Phillips made substantial offers to Frank, and it was tempting for the former migratory crop worker. But after a lot of consideration and conversations with Coach Alley, Frank chose the NBA and the Bullets.

The unprecedented salary translates into almost $89,000 in current dollars. In today's NBA, it's chicken feed. The first-round NBA draft pick for the 2014-15 season was offered a first-year salary of almost $4.6 million, with substantial increases in subsequent years.

The world of sports is one in which comparisons are constantly made. Who was the best hitter of all time? Would Babe Ruth be a star today? How many records would Ted Williams have broken had he not been called into military service twice? People will point out the differences brought about by changes in the rules or how officials make calls. These include the three-point shot, the wider lane under the basket, palming the ball and other changes intended to make the game more interesting to fans.

All of these changes had their impact, but nothing comes close to the impact made by television. The 2015 television package of the NBA infuses $24 billion into the league. Compare that with the meager amounts generated when teams were dependent on gate receipts. The value of franchises has exploded along with the value of contracts given to players. This is true in college sports as well. A check of the salaries of employees of state institutions shows that the highest paid person by far is the coach of the football and basketball teams. These things could never have happened without television.

Is this good? Some people don't think so, but fans drive the market and the money follows. People who have things to sell pitch their wares to the fan base through television, and as the profits grow the money flows into the game. Who is going to complain when the history of the league shows what happens when the money is not there? Big money generates big problems...and even scandals...but the greatness of the game and the good it has provided to so many people will weigh heavily in how these matters are judged.

The coal miner's son from Corbin, Kentucky was entering a new arena, and there would be bumps along the way.

Interruptions

Immediately after signing with the Bullets, Frank broke his ankle and couldn't play for two months. After removing the cast, he reported to Baltimore in time to join the team on a USO tour of Japan where they played exhibition games for service members.

"I couldn't jump and could only shoot," he recalled. "I developed a very painful case of shin splints which really hampered my game, but I finally played my way out of it. When we came back to Baltimore, we were joined by the other section of the team which didn't go to Japan and began our season."

The first game was against the Minneapolis Lakers, the defending national champions. Frank's entrance into the professional game was a continuation of his outstanding college years. He scored 30 points and had 15 rebounds and led the Bullets to a win over a good team. The 30 points in the first game for a rookie has only been surpassed by Wilt Chamberlain.

And then the bubble burst. "We played 11 games and were in Indiana when the coaches announced that the Bullets were out of business and in bankruptcy," Frank said. "We were told to get home on our own." Some of the guys never got paid unless they were picked up by another team.

The Milwaukee Hawks had the worst season in the league the year before so they had first pick from the Bullets' roster. Selvy was chosen first—probably the first and only time a player was the first-round draft pick two years in a row. The Hawks left Milwaukee for St. Louis, and in the second year Frank was off to a good start after playing seven games.

"We had won five of the seven and I was averaging 25 points a game and had good numbers in rebounds and assists when I got called into the Army," he said. "I went to Fort Knox and tried to play on the weekends, but it didn't work out. I would travel hard and try to get there for the game and sometimes I would get in a quarter. It didn't work out. I got in about 10 games this way."

By this time, the Korean War had ended but the Cold War with Russia was escalating. Frank would no more complain about being called into service for three years than he would boast of his game record. Just like Ted Williams and others who had their careers interrupted by military service, Frank would be the subject of speculation about what might have been had he continued the high-scoring performances of his college days. It was more than a game changer; it was a monumental life changer.

Time and place are of great importance in shaping a career and Frank was five years head of his time. His style of play was developed at Furman under a coach who recognized that the many facets of Frank's game could only be fully used when he was allowed to play from the guard position and set up the plays as a point man. This style led to his success as a scorer, and Furman had built the team around these talents. This was true upon his entrance into the professional game, when he was again the centerpiece of the offense built around his freelance style.

But things were changing fast in the basketball world and it would be different when Frank returned from the service to a game where many players had perfected the jump shot. He would have to struggle his way back into the game by using skills other than shooting and scoring.

17

Back from the Army

Frank Selvy's professional career has to be viewed in two parts. The first was the year and a half in which he entered the professional ranks and starred with the Baltimore Bullets and the Milwaukee (later St. Louis) Hawks. The second followed his call to military service. Frank has never used the interruption of his career as either an excuse or explanation in discussing the difference between the two periods.

Upon his return to the Hawks at St. Louis following three years in the service, Selvy was faced with an entirely different situation than the one he left. A number one draft pick is not left sitting on the bench. Very often there is a strong difference between the coach and the owners as to when and how to use a player, but this is not the case with a player you spent your top draft choice to get and top money to sign on. Just as it was at Furman, the Hawks coach in 1954 put Selvy in a position from which he could make maximum use of his skills. The best was when he was allowed to bring the ball up court using his ability to dribble with either hand and great speed and agility to move it quickly and gain a position from which he could fake and shoot, fake and pass, or drive the hole and suspend himself in the air from where he could lay the ball in from either side. The slam dunk was not allowed at this time but the shooter could reach over the rim and drop the ball in.

The fans loved it. The sponsors loved it. It was good business and brought in the paying customers, much to the delight of those who had invested their capital in team ownership.

In Milwaukee it was the custom of Blatz Beer to give free cases to the leading scorer, so when Frank came home from a road trip there were always a number of cases on the porch. Roger Thompson, his teammate from Furman, had returned from Korea to his home state of Wisconsin and was in the ice cream business. He was sharing an apartment with Selvy and says that they used the cases of beer to fashion tables and chairs to furnish their Spartan living quarters. Of course, they consumed their share of "the furniture" with a lot of friends who loved to visit. It was a good time in Frank's career and he was at the top of his game. The Hawks moved to St. Louis and the good life continued…and then the Army called. It's worth repeating that many top athletes have had their game interrupted and it always came with a price.

Frank spent most of his military service in Germany, after which he returned to the Hawks. Men who serve in the military are happy to come home, but rarely are they welcomed with a brass band and parade, and neither was Selvy. Professional athletes are often caught in the middle in a struggle between the owner and the coach, each of whom has his own ideas on how the team should be run and which players to use. His first year back was 1957 and he spent most of the year on the bench.

Why?

You could answer this by saying that the coach had rebuilt his team and changed his strategy and you would be right. You could also say that the injury Selvy suffered doing the broad jump in an

Army track meet in Germany was a contributing factor. You would be right again, but not entirely. Any time a player is hurt it affects his game but professional athletes become accustomed to playing through pain. The truth is that Frank was ready and only needed the confidence that is acquired through playing time to regain his form. This did not happen with the Hawks who, after a year, traded him to the New York Knicks for a shamefully low price.

A coal miner's son from the Appalachian Plateau may be quiet to the extent of appearing to be shy but he brings with him the same pride which drove him to be successful in the first place. The trade could be compared to relegating a leading actor to a walk-on role after he won an Oscar. This quiet man may not show it but the hurt is there and this rekindles his desire to rise again to the top...and Selvy did. Not in the same manner as before, because he was never given the free range that had enabled him to be the best of his time, but there were occasions when he was inserted in a game and delighted his still substantial fan base and the sports writers.

As a role player, Selvy was valuable in that he could bring the ball up and dish it off. He could be assigned to guard a leading scorer and he would cover him like a cheap suit. Regardless of how he was played, he was always a favorite with the fans.

Shortly after coming to New York and the Knicks, Frank was given an opportunity to demonstrate to the Hawks that he still had talent and cause them some remorse about failing to recognize it... or at least give it a try. The Hawks were coming to Madison Square Garden, scene of Selvy's stellar performances as a Furman Paladin. The result was thus described by sports writer Leonard Koppett in the *New York Post* on November 14, 1958:

Everyone connected with the Knicks feels wonderful today, but Frank Selvy most of all. He tasted revenge by sparking the rout of the team that scorned him, he earned the applause of a crowd ready and anxious to accept him as a hero and, most important, he showed himself how good he still is.

His even disposition and deep pride made his emotional ordeal and crises of confidence of last year all the more serious. And the situation he stepped into last night lumped everything into one package; his first real appearance as a Knick on the court that helped make him famous in the first place, playing against the Hawks, who thought so little of him that they never used him, traded him away twice for nothing in return, and won a world championship without him. "Sure, I'd been looking forward to this one," he admitted.

Frank didn't get into the game until early in the second quarter. The Knicks had played well, but the score was close. Selvy immediately hit one of his typical jump shots, and then drove in for a three pointer. Selvy, playing only 23 minutes, scored 16 points and sparked the fast break with good passing and ball swiping. Carl Braun, the teammate for whom Frank was substituted, said: "People call him just a shooter, but he's a fine all around ball player and we're lucky to have him."

The Knicks gave him a needed boost and the fans at Madison Square Garden embraced him again. As important as the game was, it was also the place where he would receive the greatest and lasting reward of his life when his friend and fellow All-American from LSU, Bob Petit, introduced him to the lovely former Miss Arkansas and runner-up Miss America, Barbara Banks, who was pursuing her career on the New York stage.

18

The New Highlight—and the Best

She came on the scene through the thoughtfulness of a fellow player and good friend, Bob Petit. Selvy and Petit were on the 1954 All-American Team and after taking different routes found themselves together on the St. Louis Hawks roster after Frank's tour in the Army. Barbara Banks was on the New York stage performing with "Your Hit Parade" and was making her success as a dancer and actress after being a top contender in the Miss America pageant as Miss Arkansas. They met on a blind date arranged by Petit through a friend from LSU who roomed with Barbara.

They were fixed up in a blind date by a former teammate, and she first saw him from the dizzying heights of Madison Square Garden. Worried that he was "short," she rushed home and changed into flats. She barely reached his shoulder.

Barbara's first view of Frank was from high up in Madison Square Garden, and from there Selvy appeared to be short, especially when he at six foot four stood next to Petit, who was six foot eleven, so she rushed back to her apartment to put on lower shoes. She had seen his picture, which was prominently displayed on the wall of the Garden, but pictures can be misleading and from where she was seated he appeared to be small. It was not necessary, of course, and she found herself standing just below his shoulders when they were introduced.

Here were two people who had arrived at this point in their lives because of their focus and dedication to their careers, but the chemistry was right...it didn't take long for Selvy to become dedicated to a new career, and it was one that would last for life. Dan Foster was a close personal friend of Frank's, a Furman graduate, and a nationally acclaimed sports writer for the *Greenville News*. This is how he announced the happy event in 1959 to the locals, including many female Selvy admirers:

BELLS FOR SELVY

At the risk of casting a gray spell throughout the YWCA and other places housing Greenville's young womanhood, it becomes our duty today to confirm that Franklin Delano Selvy will be married on the 24th of April.

It may not have been considered by some, but the greatest scorer in college basketball history had a few odd dozen fairer admirers who didn't care whether he could outscore Miss Arkansas of 1956. Well, as a matter of fact, she's the one. By name, Miss Barbara Banks of Conway, Arkansas.

The formal announcement must be reserved for its proper place on the society page, but until that one comes along,

Married on on April 15, 1959, the Selvys' "career" as man and wife is at the top of their achievements.

the informal one will do.

It came by telephone and in rather unique wording from Syracuse, New York yesterday, where Franklin was resting for last night's New York-Boston basketball game. Advised that some things had been heard concerning him down here, "How does she look?" he was asked.

"She's tough," said FDS in a majestic confirmation that he would indeed be betrothed, as reports had indicated. Miss Banks and Selvy have been engaged since Christmas Day, although they became acquainted last season through the good offices of Bob Petit, Selvy's St. Louis teammate at that time.

The article went on to discuss Barbara's role with "Your Hit Parade" and a USO tour of Korea.

Everyone knows how important it is to be successful in your career, and in sports your success—or lack of it—is widely known. The highlights of a spectacular college career and then the changes brought about by the interruption by military service and the new role he played upon his return…all of these were known. Being a No. 1 draft pick was important in launching his career but *his* No. 1 pick in choosing who would share his life and career was even more important. The time on the court or stage is relatively short and the marriage contract is forever. It was, and is, a strong union sufficient to see them through the good times and the deep wounds suffered by parents who experience the loss of a child.

There were four children, three daughters and one son. Lisa was born in 1960, Lauren in 1961, Valerie in 1963 and Mike in 1967. At the time of this writing, the Selvys have 11 grandchildren and two great-grandchildren. They lost Lauren in 1998 and Lisa in 2003. It takes monumental strength to live through these great misfortunes and a strong marriage is where you find such strength.

Mike Selvy is a commercial pilot and exceptional athlete. He displayed his talents in high school and college where he stood out in both basketball and golf. Valerie and her husband live in Greenville, where he owns and runs a sporting goods store. The Selvys are a golfing family and both Frank and Barbara are admired and appreciated by old and new friends on and off the golf course. Their careers required real physical ability and the carry over shows in their game. Don't offer to lift her golf bag…she does it herself.

19

Joining the Lakers

Frank Selvy experienced many ups and downs in his game as he was traded around from one team and system to another, all the while enduring the disappointment of not being played. In New York he had shown that he still had the ability and only needed the playing time, but these opportunities were sporadic and he never settled into an acceptable role. He was finally able to find this role with the Minneapolis Lakers, which he joined in 1959.

In Minneapolis the Lakers were well supported and Frank was well received by a team that had a place for him and wanted him. The players liked Minneapolis and were happy there. The Selvys, now a family, settled in and life leveled out.

He found his game again and demonstrated once more that he could still put the ball in the net. The following quote from an article in the *Minneapolis Morning Tribune* of March 14, 1959 describes it:

> *Vern Mikkelsen, former Minneapolis Laker great, was talking in the Laker locker room Sunday following their 114-99 victory over Detroit that gave Coach Jim Pollard's men the fifth-round playoff title:*
>
> *"Frank Selvy played like he did when he was with Milwaukee his first year in pro ball," said Mick. "He was*

impossible to stop then and today (Sunday) he had that old confidence and was shooting as he did as a rookie."

Selvy, who started the 1958-59 season with the New York Nicks and then went to Syracuse before joining the Lakers, said his 30-point total was the highest since his first year in the league. The former Furman great averaged 19 points that year and he was rated one of the best in the NBA.

"This is the best game I've played since I was discharged from the Army," said Selvy. "My big problem has been not playing. My timing was off. Now I've got it back again.'

On February 25, 1960, Frank got another boost from his adopted second state when he was named Player of the Decade for the Carolinas by a distinguished panel of coaches, including Lyles Alley. He led the balloting with 2,538 points or an average of 32.5 points per game per year for three years, followed by Dick Groat of Duke, 22.8; Len Rosenbuth of North Carolina, 26.9; Dick Hemric of Wake Forest, 24.9; and Grady Wallace of University of South Carolina, 28. Other contenders were Ron Shavlik, Lou Pucillo, and Dick Dickey of North Carolina State, and three Furman players, Darrell Floyd, Raeford Well, and L. Rhyne.

When notified by telephone of the panel's choice, Frank said simply, "That's wonderful. I'm honored." Coach Alley was more expressive. "I'm truly happy about this," he told the *Charlotte Observer*. Frank was a great player and a great person. He came a long way and all the honors he won never changed him one bit. He was a clean living person both on and off the court and was never known to question an official's decision or become involved in any arguments with spectators or players."

This is the kind of praise that could be applied only to those who had the skills and character to become a "credit to the game."

The Lakers in L.A.

The Lakers organization moved the team to Los Angeles prior to the 1961 season for the same reason the baseball Giants and Dodgers did. The market was bigger and professional basketball, like professional baseball, is a business. Again, the reader is reminded that the pre-television business of sports was dependent on gate receipts and whatever revenue could be generated locally. Los Angeles was an attractive place to be and the high-profile Lakers players were recognized and

1960-61 LOS ANGELES LAKERS

Jerry West   Rod Hundley   Ron Johnson   Tom Hawkins   Frank Selvy   Bob Leonard
Coach   Trainer
Fred Schaus   Elgin Baylor   Jim Krebs   Ray Felix   Rudy LaRusso   Howard Jolliff   Frank O'Neill

Lakers 1960-61 Team Photo. Frank is second from the right, back row.

treated especially well by the fans. The all-important revenue stream improved. Naturally, they retained their name, even though Los Angeles, unlike Minneapolis, is not situated on the shores of a Great Lake.

It was different now for Selvy. He had viewed the game from the top. He had been the leading scorer and had seen his name in print from coast to coast and these things never changed his personality or values from what he had brought with him from his mountain background. He had felt the bitter disappointment of riding the bench and being traded around in a manner which reflected the low regard some owners and coaches had for his ability after he left the service. He retained his skills and pride even when he was being minimized or ignored. Now he was with a team where he could get back into the game he loved.

He was a family man now and the game was his way of supporting his family. These would be good years and happy ones. He was where he could once again enjoy playing with teammates who were also friends and before knowledgeable fans who admired his style of play. Some of the fans were prominent Hollywood stars who became Selvy fans…fans of both Frank and Barbara. The singer and actress Doris Day, who was at the peak of her outstanding career, would sit with Barbara during the games and they would be joined by actor James Garner and entertainer Pat Boone.

Teammate Jerry West became a good friend. They had a lot in common: they came from similar backgrounds and were typically quiet and private. They had similar physiques and styles of play and made an ideal pair of guards for Los Angeles. It was a good fit for Frank to be inserted into a guard role working in support of West and Elgin Baylor... both of whom he liked and admired. Those who love the game want above all else just to play. The good ones always want to be the best but, more than that, they want to be a good teammate and to win.

Frank as a guard with the Lakers, setting up a play against the New York Knicks.

Shooting would always be a valuable part of the Selvy game but he never was without the other skills that a good team needs, so it was a source of pride and pleasure to be assigned a defensive role. To shut down the best scorer of the opposing team became a welcomed assignment as was the role of ball handling and dishing off to West and Baylor, who were looked to for the point making. On the court and off he was happy being a Laker.

A game that has been rehashed and talked about for years was played in 1962. It was Game 7 of the NBA finals and the Lakers faced a four-point deficit at the hands of the Boston Celtics as the clock was down to the final minute of the game's fourth quarter. Selvy then proceeded to pull down two crucial rebounds and scored two baskets to tie the game at 100. Just before the buzzer, the Lakers once again regained possession and raced towards the Celtics' goal. Rod Hundley had the ball. West and Baylor were covered and Hundley had the option to either shoot the ball or pass it off to Selvy. He chose the latter. The shot was a 12- footer that would have secured the championship for the Lakers had it gone in.

It didn't happen. The ball hit the cylinder and rimmed out. It would have been the ultimate heroic moment, but this time it went out. Replays show that Bob Cousey, who was guarding Frank, hit his arm on the follow-through but this was missed by the officials.

Why was this shot so remembered? Because it sent the game into overtime where the Celtics prevailed, and this was the second of seven NBA Finals match-ups between Boston and Los Angeles over the course of 11 seasons. The Lakers ultimately lost every one of those championship battles with the Celtics and this multiplied the pain of missing a golden opportunity. Selvy's shot would have prevented that streak of futility from happening. People remember the missed shot but not the two rebounds and baskets that tied the game and set the stage for it to happen. No one has to remind Frank of the shot because he remembers it well…along with probably every other shot he ever took.

"Hot Rod" Hundley, who passed the ball to Frank, took great pleasure in bringing it up and needling him about it. Hundley had a totally different approach to the game than Frank. He liked to joke and play, even at serious times, and this was a puzzle to the sober-minded Selvy to whom every move was a serious matter and a missed shot a painful experience.

Regrets? Yes…he's sorry he didn't make the shot. Was he sorry he had taken it rather than to have passed it off? No. He had his chance and he took it. He wanted it that way and no other way.

The reader is reminded of the dramatic scene in the movie *On the Waterfront* when Marlon Brando lamented his regrets about his ring career: "I cudda been a contender…I cudda been somebody." The good ones want the chance which is why a missed opportunity is more painful to them than the pain of a missed shot.

Elgin Baylor, who was positioning himself for the rebound when Selvy launched the shot, had this to say: "Selvy, a two-time NBA

Frank Selvy, Fred Schaus (Coach), Wayne Embry,
Oscar Robertson, Elgin Baylor, GeneShue, Bob Pettit,
Cliff Hagan, Jerry West, Jack Twyman, Bailey Howell, Walt Bellamy

1962 WEST NBA ALL STAR

1962 West NBA All-Star Team. Frank is at far left.

All-Star, is a very good person. He's a good guy, but Frank is very sensitive about things, and he's not the type of person that likes to be teased about anything." Anyone who has ever visited the mountains of Kentucky knows people like this.

Selvy, who played six of his nine NBA seasons with the Lakers, also knows that no one shot makes or breaks an entire series. He thinks the Lakers should have won the championship in Game 6, when they took an early lead before Boston roared back in the third quarter and blew them out, 119-105. He's still mystified as to why he spent much of that game on the bench, watching Hundley play in his place.

"We were up 3-2 in the series and it was back in L.A.," Selvy recalled of Game 6. "I was 5 for 5 from the field and was guarding Sam Jones and he hadn't scored a point. We had a 17-point lead. Then I get put on the bench, and by the time I come back in we're down by 10. Maybe Hot Rod can explain that."

Boston won 11 titles between 1957 and 1969. "It could possibly have changed things," Baylor said. "We always thought that we could win. We never thought we were going to lose. We just felt that we were good enough to win."

Frank felt the same way. He says that, despite the teasing, he owes Hundley a small debt of gratitude: "He's kept my name in print."

21

Selvy's Chilling Thrill

A professional player leads an exciting life both on the court and off. The Selvys, along with several other Laker families, rented housing in a quiet neighborhood and became closely knit. Cookouts together with the children and outings at the beach and in the many Los Angeles area parks were very welcome for Barbara, who had spent so much of their newly married life alone. When Lisa was born in Syracuse, Barbara was alone so they kept her in the hospital for almost a week until Frank came home from a road trip. Now, when the team was away the ladies babysat each other's children and spent a lot of time together.

Sportswriter Dan Foster relates an event from that time which he titled "Selvy's Chilling Thrill." Here's the way he reported it in the *Greenville News*:

> *Frank Selvy has been asked, literally hundreds of times, 'What was your greatest thrill in basketball?' and for the past six years the answer has been the same. "The night my family came down and saw me," Selvy has always responded. That was the night in which he scored 100 points against Newberry.*
>
> *Last night in the Fellowship Hall of Trinity Methodist Church, Frank admitted rather under his breath another*

incident. "That was my greatest thrill." It takes nothing away from devotion to parents or the Golden Era of Textile Hall. It was simply a way of saying that being alive has to be a greater thrill than anything you do while you are alive.

"That night," Selvy relates of the [1960] crash landing of the Minneapolis Lakers team airplane, "we all thought we had had it."

Basically poised and calm, Franklin still gets very animated when he discusses it. The occasion of last night's re-telling was a banquet honoring the Senior and Intermediate teams of Trinity Methodist Church.

He got undivided attention. Come to think of it, you don't find people on every corner who can tell you how it feels to be in an airplane mishap.

'We Were Following a Car'

"We were just a few minutes out of St. Louis on a Sunday night," he began of the incident in January.

"The electrical system failed and we had no radio, no heat, and no compass. We couldn't go back to St. Louis without a radio to tell them we were in trouble, they wouldn't know to clear the field for us and we may have collided with another plane.

"The temperature must have been nearly zero. Everyone in the plane was freezing, but we didn't think much about it, because there was too much else to worry about."

Selvy said the plane descended very slowly. It was three or four hours, he related, from the time they knew they were in peril until they came to a safe stop in an Iowa cornfield.

"*It was snowing, a real snow storm, and the windshield wipers weren't working so the pilots had to stick their heads out of the window to see anything at all. We got down to about 200 feet, I thought. We almost hit a water tank once. The pilots were looking for a field, maybe even an airport they could land it in.*

"*We were obviously lost. Once I saw a car down on the road and we were following it, just above it. When it turned left, we turned left. When it turned right, we turned right. Once it started up a hill and we shot right into a sharp climb.*

"*I can see that fellow now when he got home or wherever he was going. I bet he walked in and said, 'I know you don't believe me but an airplane started following me and almost hit me. Okay, so you don't believe me!'*

Missed a Fence on Landing

"*Anyway, we didn't know how much gas we had, and after a while, probably four hours later, they saw a field and started circling it to take a look. I don't believe anybody on the plane thought we'd make it. There were too many things against us. I know every player on the team was scared to death.*

"*Most of them had blankets over their heads,*" Selvy added after the banquet, "*and that thing about Elgin Baylor lying down in the back of the plane and saying if we were going to crash he might as well be comfortable is just not true. That is a story that somebody told somebody else and it made the newspapers.*"

Selvy said the pilots apparently thought the cornfield would be alright, so they started the final approach.

"We just missed a fence. We landed in a lot of snow and the wheels were down. I never heard such cheering by the players at any of our games as I heard when we got out of the plane."

It was after relating the story that Frank said: "that was my greatest thrill."

A life-threatening event changes the way a person looks at life and causes him to put things in perspective. Basketball is a game, even a means of livelihood, but every player knows that there's an end to their career and most of them make preparation for that event. Life after the game is expected and even looked forward to and the event reminded a plane full of Lakers of how thankful they were for the safe landing.

Barbara was with several of the Lakers wives when the news came that the plane had crashed and was shocked, but this news was followed immediately by a telephone call from one of the players and this turned the grief into intense happiness.

22

Life After the Game

As important as playing the game was and as central its role in his life, the time came for Frank Selvy to turn the page and face the new challenges presented by his responsibilities as a family man. His name was permanently entered in the record books as the leading college player of his time and he had enjoyed a very good professional career lasting nine years, during which time he averaged 11 points a game. It was that time for the Selvys.

It turned out he had new options that were directly the result of his reputation as a player. The first and most obvious was coaching, and Furman University had every reason to welcome him back… and did. In March of 1964 he retired from the Lakers and reported to his alma mater as assistant coach for basketball. After two seasons as assistant, Frank accepted the head coach position, which he held for four years, and then he retired from basketball for good.

Some things are left behind and some are carried with you when one phase of your life ends and the scene shifts to new challenges. When the Selvys left the Lakers, the fans in Los Angeles showed their appreciation and held a party which was well attended by some Hollywood notables. Money was raised as a farewell gift and it was the plan to use it for a swimming pool, but it still remains a puzzle as to what happened to it. Some people give and some people take and some get disappointed in the process.

The Selvy drive to the basket was a compliment to Frank's other shots and would make his opponent a spectator as he either left the floor with his extraordinary leap or complete the drive by the dribble with either hand. The result was the same…another score and another roar from the crowd. These pictures demonstrate these skills.

Playing against Davidson while at Furman, Selvy is pictured suspended in air as he chooses whichever hand he will use to finish the move.

Facing the Boston Celtics, Selvy is closely guarded by K.C. Jones as he drives by using the left handed dribble, while in the background his teammate Elgin Baylor is guarded by Tom Sanders.

This picture shows the striking similarity between Frank Selvy's drive and the logo of the NBA, which is based on his teammate Jerry West. In this picture Selvy is using the right hand whereas in the logo West is using the left. They had similar physiques.

What should a few thousand dollars mean to a man who had been a star performer in the NBA for nine years? The reader is reminded that was before the vast input of money brought about by television, and though the Selvys were leaving the game better off than before they started, they were by no means set up for an early retirement. They would have to wait for the swimming pool. The game was over and memories were important, but the need to provide for the family remained and called for a new career which began with the Furman coaching job.

Coaches' salaries were minimal at the time for the same reasons that impacted on the players and owners of professional franchises: the limited amount of money generated by gate receipts. Television money was just over the horizon, but would not arrive in time to reward Frank as a player or coach. Still, a well-known reputation is an entrée into a new career, and the Selvy name still carried the same magic as it had in the 1950s.

The managers of the Saint Jo Paper Company were quick to appreciate the advantages of having a representative with such name recognition and appeal and offered Frank a job in sales. It worked from the start and for a number of years he was the leading salesman. To be sure, he didn't talk his way into such success, but a distinguished man with a quiet demeanor and a scratch golf game could sell a lot of packaging.

The Barbara Selvy Dance Studio became another valuable source of income for the family. It was directly the result of name recognition and, even more important, the talent and energy of the former stage professional and beauty queen. Where many young men and women were inspired by the performance of Frank Selvy on the basketball court, there were hundreds of young women and men drawn to the stage by Barbara Banks Selvy. Greenville was where the road to success began and where it ultimately led to a quiet retirement for the Selvys, a place where they could live out their senior years surrounded by family and friends who share their love of Furman basketball and golf.

The Selvys had four children: Lisa, Lauren, Valerie and Michael. Children are a source of great pleasure to their families but can also be the source of monumental pain. Lisa and Lauren never enjoyed good health and both died early, leaving behind them the kind of memories that can generate smiles at times and tears at others. Lauren left a two-year-old daughter, Madison, who was adopted by Frank and Barbara and became another daughter rather than a granddaughter. Valerie and Mike live in the Greenville area and they and their families remain in close contact with their parents, one of the greatest rewards of a successful life.

Those who love the game retain their attachment even when they no longer play. Just as in every other business or profession, the memories remain and come to mind often during the quiet days of retirement. The thoughtful man remembers those years of practice and training which led to his success and the people who opened doors and taught him the rules that should be followed. He grades his performance over and over in his mind and relives the thrill of a victory or the pain of a defeat. More important…he knows how he went about it. He once again recalls what the game gave to him and what he gave to the game.

Frank Selvy was a credit to the game. Some play the game and some work the game. Some inspire others with a display of honest modesty and team spirit that instills a pride in his teammates and honor to his institution. The lad or lass on the playground wants to make the team…then become the best…and in the process they derive pleasure from their efforts. When this happens, they feel pride of accomplishment and makes their family proud. They do it for the school and wear their block letters proudly to let everyone know who they are and who they play for. We've all seen it; their town wants to honor them.

In his great poem "To the Athlete Who Died Young," A.E. Housman wrote these introductory lines:

> *The day you won our town the race we chaired you through the market place.*
> *Men and boys stood cheering by as home we brought you shoulder high.*

How often this scene is replayed all over the country—and it never loses its appeal. Winning the race for your town or school affords a thrill in athletics that can't be duplicated by monetary rewards. Playing the game better than others and with honor and ethics serves as an inspiration to those coming along behind you and makes the game better than it was before you played. The purity of the game is preserved and you made your contribution. This is what is meant when it is said that the only true measure of the player can be made by those who saw him when the lights in the arena were on and he was on the stage.

Each generation produces a new crop of such stars and they all deserve to be remembered for what they added to the way the game should be played. The good one elevates the game and becomes a rung on the ladder. There were many occasions when the coal miner's son found himself being carried shoulder high to the cheers of the men and boys made happy by the game.

It has to be remembered that it's a game... a great game... but a game nonetheless. It brings pleasure to those who play it and to those who are spectators

The picture here shows Frank with some of his former teammates from the Hawks organization: Bob Petit, Ned Parks, and Ed McCauley witness Frank's tee shot. A look at his face reveals the seriousness with which Selvy approaches the game.

and for some it brings fame and fortune. It has brought recognition to the institutions that recruited the players, hired the coaches and built the coliseums, and for some this is not good. Those who were and are a credit to the game should be recognized and applauded and those who have created shadows of suspicion and doubt should also be recognized...and judged accordingly.

Teams, coaches and institutions and everyone associated with basketball have been influenced by the massive amounts of money generated. Corporations have cashed in on the opportunity to push their products...and so have colleges. Fans have gone beyond all reason in their celebrations after a win or in their rage after a loss and expressed themselves by overturning automobiles belonging to people they don't even know. They do these things in the name of sports or the honor of their school or city. It's worth repeating...that is why it's so important to uphold and remember those individuals and institutions that have done it well.

Afterword and Acknowledgements

Among the benefits derived from a long life is the pleasure afforded by friendships. New friends are always welcome but an old friendship, like good wine, is enhanced by aging and the good times become better through years of memory and the retelling of the events. Such is the group of central characters who make up the cast of players in the story of *Frank Selvy: Coal Miner's Son*. Each generation produces some who are not only different, but unique, and this writer has been blessed by having been close to many of them for more than 60 years.

Some have said that this book should have been written 40 years ago and this is true, but in that event this writer would not have been considered for the honor and for that reason alone casts a dissenting vote. To have been asked by Barbara Banks Selvy and Franklin D. himself to make the attempt set the stage for a revisit to a period of time during which the game of basketball made significant moves that improved the game for the players and spectators is a great honor. These events tell a story that any real student of the game should appreciate.

The writer makes some claims that may be challenged and sincerely hopes they are. The claim that Frank Selvy invented the jump shot stands out as an invitation to any student of the game to issue his challenge. The jump shot is such an integral part of the game today that it's difficult to imagine a time when it was not…but there was. Tall players mostly used the hook and layup and the short players mostly used the two-handed set shot.

It's also important to look at and discuss the impact of television and the vast amount of money it generates. Frank has to be included among those who made the game more attractive to fans and television.

Frank Selvy was the best. No claim is made that he is the best of all time because that claim could never be successfully made about any player. It's enough to say that Selvy was the best of *his* time, and the record shows it.

The title of this book invites the reader to think in depth about how the game provides an avenue on which the ambitions of talented and dedicated young players can travel and, in the process, find a world where they reap great rewards for their efforts. This was the route traveled by Franklin D. Selvy, the coal miner's son, which led him from the poverty of the Appalachian Plateau to the bright lights of big cities where he enjoyed the admiration of movie stars and other celebrities. This is also the route traveled by Loretta Lynn, the coal miner's daughter, whose talent led to a different career, but the beginning and routes were very much alike.

As stated in the preface, this book is about basketball and a lot more. It's also about Furman University, small but highly respected by those who recognize the value of high social and academic standards; and Greenville, South Carolina, small as cities go but great in the things that make life enjoyable. Furman and Greenville were the perfect place for Frank Selvy to establish his reputation.

In reviewing the writing of this book, it became obvious that it is not as much a creative effort by the author as it was a compilation of information gathered from family and friends, assembled into manuscript form and polished into book form by an editor and advisor. My pride in the effort comes from having been honored with the opportunity to do it.

Furman University has a very good and cooperative archives department.

Teammates of Frank's have been enthusiastic in their sharing. Roger Thompson, Nield Gordon and Bobby Chambers stand out in this regard.

Kathryn Smith has edited and advised me on my previous books and did it again. She deserves special thanks.

Dick Riley and Blackie Cook gave their perspective as classmates and friends at Furman. Jerry West enriched the book with his appreciative words about his friend and teammate with the Los Angeles Lakers.

Finally, and by no means of less importance, is the friendship I have enjoyed with Frank and all of the above, starting with my years at Furman as a classmate and extending to this very day.

About the Author

Jack McIntosh grew up on the Cooper River side of downtown Charleston and attended the public schools there. He was a corporal in the United States Marine Corps, after which he graduated from Furman University. He served in the army during the Korean Conflict as a tank platoon leader, then graduated from the law school at the University of South Carolina. Jack practiced law in Anderson, South Carolina for more than fifty years as a "small town lawyer," and continues living there in retirement. His previous books are *Don't Kill ALL the Lawyers…I'll give you a short list*, which was read on NPR's "Radio Reader" by Dick Estell; and *Ain't Mad at Nobody*. Jack's books are available on amazon.com